GIFTS

WITHIN THE

Gift

A GUIDE TO HELP YOU ACTIVATE
YOUR GIFT WITHIN THE MINISTRY

GIFTS

within the

Gift

Helen Speights & Harlene Pruitt

Copyright ©2017 by Helen Speights and Harlene Pruitt

Published by Extreme Overflow Publishing
A division of Extreme Overflow Enterprises, Inc
Grayson, Georgia 30017
www.extremeoverflow.com

Cover by James Nesbit www.jnesbit.com

All rights reserved.
This book or parts thereof may not be reproduced in
any form, stored in a retrieval system or transmitted in
any form by any means-electronic, mechanical,
photocopy, recording or otherwise.

Unless otherwise noted, all Scripture quotations are
taken from the Life Application Study Bible, New
International Version.

Manufactured in the United States of America
10 9 8 7 6 5 4 3 2 1

ISBN 978-0-9989351-1-9

Dedication

We dedicate this book to Elohim 'God' of revelation
and His manifest glory to all who read this book.
Also, we invite all those that are thirsty for more of
God, to come and drink from this oasis book,
Gifts within the gift.

TABLE OF CONTENTS

h. Importance of Seeking the Face of
   God

Chapter 16: Final Closing Chapter

Chapter 17: From the heart of Prophet Helen

Chapter 18: From the heart of Prophet Harlene

Appendix

   a. Special notes on Prophecy
   b. Activations
   c. Prophetic Activations
   d. Testimonies of Activations
   e. Eleven Things to Remember
   f. Pictures of Activation
   g. Information Sheet
   h. Prophetic Book Covering
      Meaning

INTRODUCTION

My twin, Harlene and I, were preparing for a prophetic conference. We prayed to God for His revelatory knowledge to obtain different material for this prophetic event. We also prayed to God for His revelatory knowledge on how to present this information in a training format. God gave us material and through the Holy Spirit informed us to turn it into a book. We Praise the Lord that He responded quickly in answering us!

Gifts within the Gift is a title designed to make a person think. This is exactly what we want the reader to do. Through a moment of pondering, we want the reader to obtain knowledge of the Gifts within the gift. It's equally important for the reader to also learn the operations of the Gift within the gifts as well. God's word warns us that people are destroyed for lack of knowledge (Hosea 4:6). God does not want his people ignorant of the possession and the operation of the Gifts within the Gift.

The gift is Jesus Christ. In Hebrew, the name Jesus Christ means Yeshua Hamashiach "Jesus the Messiah." The name Jesus is the Greek form of the Hebrew name Yeshua, which is the shortened form of the name Yehoshua. From this Hebrew word we also get the name Joshua (Joshua 5:15) or Hoshea (Numbers 13:8; Deuteronomy 33:44). The name means "salvation" and is found more than often throughout the Old Testament. This is the name from which we get the Greek word Iesous, pronounced "yay-sus," or as we say it, "Jesus." The J did not get added to the Hebrew alphabet until 1524, however, before that they used the letter I.

The word 'gifts' in the Greek is 'charismata' and relates to the grace (charis) of God. This meaning also represents 'gifts of grace, to show favor, free gifts, an undeserved benefit.' The Gifts of the Holy Spirit are the accurate knowledge of remarkable powers by the Holy Spirit to the believer for the manifestation of a gift for the edification of others. This is God's favor; we did not earn these gifts but we accept them by faith.

Throughout the scriptures, there is evidence of the gift of the Holy Spirit. In the book of John 14:26, Jesus asked God to release the Holy Spirit to teach us all things and remind us of everything Jesus said (when he taught here on earth). Also, in Acts chapter 2, Peter informs the people to receive the gift of the Holy Spirit. For this gift of promise (the Holy Spirit) is for you and for your children, and for all who are afar off, as many as the Lord our God will call.

The Holy Spirt brought His gifts with Him; it was one gift that came down from God, because God is one. Further, the one Gift, the Holy Spirit came from the Father, God. He in turn, disperses His nine gifts to the believers. The Holy Spirit' nine gifts have three distinct qualities; Revelation, Power and Communication. Each of these qualities having three distinctions within them. Additionally, let us not take lightly the seven symbols of the Holy Spirit that aid us in the possession and operation of the Gift.

Finally, let the body of Christ remember Jesus Christ and the Holy Spirit as the gift that dwells within us. Therefore, we were given a gift also acknowledging we are the gift to release gifts through the Holy Spirit, in order to demonstrate the kingdom of God on the earth.

CHAPTER I

Now concerning spiritual gifts, brethren, I do not

want you to be ignorant.

(1 Corinthians 12:1)

The gift of Holy Spirit informs us of spiritual things. In the scripture above; as Apostle Paul tells the church, do not to be ignorant of them (spiritual things). The word ignorance in Greek is 'agnoia.' The original word 'ignorant' in Greek is 'agnoeo,' meaning to be ignorant of, unknown, without knowledge, not to know, not to understand, to mistake, be wrong. Therefore, the Holy Spirit is stating in that one word, 'agnoeo,' do not lack knowledge or be uninformed about spiritual gifts.

There are two kinds of ignorance also known as 'agnoia,' (or ignorant 'agnoeo').

1. Ignorance towards the knowledge of the Gifts within the Gift.

2. Ignorance towards the operation of the Gifts within the Gift.

Vignette #1 - Annie & the Nursing Home

Annie Johnson lived in a poverty stricken, semi-private nursing home in Chicago. Each month her pastor, Bill, would visit her by driving to the facility at 6pm every Thursday. On Thursday, the pastor entered Annie's room with a hello and sat down near the night table close to her bed. Immediately he noticed papers that looked like legal documents and decided to ask Annie if she knew what the documents were. She replied that her late husband left those papers but did not have the opportunity to explain them to her before he passed. Pastor asked Annie's permission to take the legal document to his lawyer. Annie agreed and gave her pastor the documents. Within three days, pastor Bill returned with his lawyer, Mr. Smith and informed Annie what the documents meant. The documents stated that Annie's husband paid for her to live in a luxurious senior living facility in downtown Chicago. By doing so she would have a tremendous amount of finances left over. Annie cried, rejoiced and moved from the facility she was in to the luxury facility that was already paid for on her behalf.

There are many, like Annie, who are ignorant of their rightful possessions. Annie could have been living in luxury but instead she lived in poverty for many years. Annie's story is a mere illustration of how ignorance of our possession; 'Jesus Christ & Holy Spirit' as a GIFT can cost us dearly.

Vignette #2 - Susan & the Guitar

A young eight year old girl, named Susan was fascinated with her older brother's guitar. One day she saw her brother's guitar lying on his bed. She went into his room, picked up the guitar and started pulling on the strings. To her surprise a guitar string broke. She threw the guitar back on the bed and ran out of the room. When her brother returned home and found out his guitar string was broken he was furious because it was going to cost him a lot of money to repair.

There are many like Susan who lack knowledge of the operation of an instrument. Susan's story is an illustration of how ignorance of the operation of the gifts within the gift; along with understanding the power in what we possess, can cost us.

It is imperative that we study the gifts within the Gift to show ourselves approved by God, rightly dividing the word of truth. Further, until their functions manifest in us and through us:

1. One must have the determination to possess the knowledge and operation of the Holy Spirit; The Gift "Jesus Christ & Holy Spirit."

2. One must learn to yield to the Holy Spirit, flow with the Holy Spirit, and make ourselves available for the manifestation of His spiritual gifts.

3. One must have the tenacity to operate in the function of the Holy Spirit; which is in the spiritual gifts, for the glory of God and not self-seeking.

CHAPTER 2

THE PROMISE

Through the power of the gifts within the gift of
Jesus Christ and the Holy Spirit, God makes four
promises.

Promise #1: The Holy Spirit

*Therefore being exalted to the right hand of God,
and having received from the Father; the promise of
the Holy Spirit, He poured out this which you now
see and hear. "For David did not ascend into the
heavens, but he says himself: 'The Lord said to my
Lord, 'Sit at My right hand, Till I make Your
enemies Your footstool." "Therefore let all the
house of Israel know assuredly that God has made
this Jesus, whom you crucified, both Lord and
Christ." Now when they heard this, they were cut to*

the heart, and said to Peter and the rest of the apostles, "Men and brethren, what shall we do?" Then Peter said to them, "Repent, and let every one of you be baptized in the name of Jesus Christ for the remission of sins; and you shall receive the gift of the Holy Spirit. For the promise is to you and to your children, and to all who are afar off, as many as the Lord our God will call." Acts 2:33-39

Promise #2: Ability to do even greater things

Just as the Lord Jesus informed His disciples, He assures us, "most solemnly I tell you, if anyone steadfastly believes in Me, he will himself be able to do the things that I do; and he will do even greater things than these, because I go to the Father," (John 14:12, AMP).

Promise #3: Signs and wonders will follow

In the scriptures His promise continues by saying, "And these signs will follow those who believe: In My name they will cast out demons; they will speak with new tongues; they will take up serpents; and if they drink anything deadly, it will by no means hurt them; they will lay hands on the sick, and they will recover," (Mark 16:17-18).

Promise #4: Power from on high

God's power from on high is displayed as a promise in this scripture, "Behold, I send the promise of My Father upon you; but tarry in the city of Jerusalem until you are endured with power from on high. But you shall receive power when the Holy Spirit has come upon you; and you shall be witnesses to Me in Jerusalem, and in all Judea and

Samaria, and to the end of the earth" (Luke 24:49; Acts 1:8).

The Lord Jesus Christ promises to the kingdom of God are not just talk. They are the evidence that follows behind God's power (1 Corinthians 4:20). We see this in the scriptures in Acts 3:1-16 where Peter and John demonstrated the power of God at the beautiful temple gate.

Another example of the manifestation of God's promises happen at the water baptism Jesus received. Through the Holy Spirit, the Lord Jesus himself, prayed for the promise of the Father (Isaiah 11:1-2; 61:1-2). Having received the promise, He then went about teaching the commandments of God, preaching the goodness of God and healing all those oppressed of the devil (Matthew 4:23; 9:35; Mark 6:56; Luke 4:1,14; 8:1; Acts 10:38).

Without the Holy Spirt and His power, Jesus Christ ministry would not have been effective. He prayed for the promise of the Holy Spirt (Luke 3:21). After receiving the promise, He went out preaching and teaching the kingdom of God. With power, He healed all of those who were oppressed by the devil (Matthew 4:23; 9:35; Mark 6:56). How much more do believers need the (Gift of the) Holy Spirit and its power to present His glory to the kingdom of God?

CHAPTER 3

THE NEED OF THE GIFT

Then Peter said to them, "Repent, and let every one of you be baptized in the name of Jesus Christ for the remission of sins; and you shall receive the gift of the Holy Spirit.

Acts 2:38

Do we receive the spiritual gifts of the Holy Spirit or gift the Holy Spirit? Another way to think about this questions is, Would a sinner need Jesus Christ or salvation? Clearly, he/she would need the Lord Jesus Christ who is our savior (Matthew 1:21; Jn 1:29; 1 Jn 3:5). Jesus Christ, is the gift that came down from heaven (John 3:16; 4:10; 2 Corinthians 9:15, John 1:29; 1 John 3:5). And He also brought with Him gifts of eternal life, truth, mercy, grace, righteousness and more (John 1:17; Romans 5:15, 17; 6:23). What is keeping you from the gift?

CHAPTER 4

THE GIFTS IN THE GIFT

Gifts of the Spirit are given to unite the body of Christ. Jesus, the gift, prayed to Abba Father for Him to release His Holy Spirit. Jesus asked Him to send His Spirit to them. So, Jesus and the Holy Spirit would dwell within them always, along with the spiritual gifts (Psalms 68:18; John 14:16, 18; 15:26; Ephesians 4:8).

When the Holy Spirit came to dwell in us at the baptism of the Holy Spirit, He also brought His gifts with Him. It was one gift that came down from God, because God is one (Ephesians 4:6). Further, when the one Gift, Holy Spirit came from Abba

Father, He dispersed nine gifts to the believer (Acts 10:45; 11:17; 1 Corinthians 12:11).

The gift; the Holy Spirit, that came down on the day of Pentecost (Acts 2:1) was the same Spirit of God who poised over the waters at creation (Genesis 1:3). This same Spirit enabled Moses to part the Red Sea and helped him to communicate with God face to face (Exodus 14:21; 33:11). Further, the Holy Spirit enabled us to speak with God through unknown tongues (1 Corinthians 14:2). Also, the same Holy Spirit came upon Samson (Judge 13:25; 14:6), Elisha in double measure (2 Kings 2:9-13), John the Baptist in his mother's womb (Luke 1:15) and upon the Lord Jesus at His baptism (Matthew 3:16). This same Holy Spirit comes upon us today when we are filled with the Holy Spirit (Acts 2:4). How awesome!

CHAPTER 5

SYMBOLS OF THE HOLY SPIRIT

In relationship to the Holy Spirit' presence that manifests his anointing in our lives, we need to correlate the symbols that represent the Holy Spirit.

Below is not a conclusive list; however these are a few symbols to mention.

1. **Seal**

   When you believed and become born again, you are marked with the seal of the promised Holy Spirit.

   The Holy Spirit comes within giving all believers the authority to become children of God (Ephesians 1:13; 4:30; John 1:12).

2. **Water**

   After you are sealed by the Holy Spirit, He will help you renew your mind through the washing of water by the Word of God (Ephesians 5:26 NIV).

   Whoever believes in me, as Scripture has said, rivers of living water will flow from within them (John 7:38 NIV).

3. **Fire**

   After the Holy Spirit assists you in washing and renewing your mind; with the word of God, He starts a purging, a purifying through the baptism of His fire (Matthew 3:11 NIV). This is so that you would present your bodies as living sacrifices (Romans 12:1).

   They saw what seemed to be tongues of fire that separated and came to rest on each of them (Acts 2:3 NIV).

4. Oil

God's anointing comes to help us in the five-fold ministry. Through the oil, you love righteousness and hate wickedness; therefore God, your God, has set you above your companions by anointing you with the oil of joy (Psalms 45:7b NIV).

The anointing oil flow over us saturating our spirit in the presence of God (Psalms 133:2 NIV)

5. Dove

The Holy Spirit enables the believer to glide with God in a close relationship; with the manifestation of flowing in the revelation gifts, liken to a dove. *Then John gave this testimony: I saw the Spirit come down from heaven as a dove and remain on him* (John 1:32).

6. Wind

Whether a believer realizes it not, it is no longer him that lives but Christ is truly in charge of his life. There is an intense oneness with the Lord Jesus Christ. Then the Holy Spirit manifests like a wind, assisting the believer in the power gifts (Exodus 14:21; Job 38:1).

Suddenly a sound like the blowing of a violent wind came from heaven and filled the whole house where they were sitting (Acts 2:2).

7. Cloud

Our heavenly Father manifest Himself as a cloud in Matthew 17:5 and Mark 9:7.

As Moses went into the tent, the pillar of cloud would come down and stay at the entrance, while the Lord spoke with Moses.

Whenever the people saw the pillar of cloud standing at the entrance to the tent, they all stood and worshiped each at the entrance to their tent. The Lord would speak to Moses face to face, as one speaks to a friend. Then Moses would return to the camp, but his young aide Joshua son of Nun did not leave the tent (Exodus 33:9-11).

There is a realm that the believer must fight to obtain so the manifestation of the vocal gifts can be demonstrated. Also, in order to work the miracles of Jesus one must live a life of complete dedication to God. When a believer surrenders all spirit, soul and body to God without any exception, it is the highest symbol of the gift.

CHAPTER 6

MINISTRIES GIFTS

In Ephesians 4, Paul told us that when Jesus left this earth, He gave gifts to men. These are called the ministry gifts.

These gifts were to further the plan of God through Jesus. When He ascended back to His Father, He gave some to be apostles, prophets, evangelists, pastors, and teachers to His body. The goal of the ministry was to:

a. Prepare God's people for works of service

b. Build up the body of Christ

c. Bring the body to unity in the faith

d. Teach the knowledge of the Son of God

e. Bring believers to a place of maturity

f. Bring believers to the fullness of Christ

For the equipping of the saints for the work of ministry, for the edifying of the body of Christ, till we all come to the unity of the faith and the knowledge of the Son of God, to a perfect man, to the measure of the stature of the fullness of Christ.
Ephesians 4:12, 13

The ministry gifts are appointed by God and not by the choice of men. Therefore man must flow with the Holy Spirit and not the flesh when they appoint ministers.

CHAPTER 7

DIFFERENCE OF MINISTRIES

Now there are diversities of gifts, but the same Spirit. And there are diversities of ministrations, yet the same Lord. And there are diversities of workings, but the same God, who worketh all things in all. But to each one is given the manifestation of the Spirit to profit withal. For to one is given through the Spirit the word of wisdom; and to another the word of knowledge, according to the same Spirit: to another faith, in the same Spirit; and to another gifts of healings, in the one Spirit; and to another workings of miracles; and to another prophecy; and to another discerning of spirits: to another divers kinds of tongues; and to another the interpretation of tongues: but all these worketh the one and the same Spirit, dividing to each one severally even as he will.

1 Corinthians 12:4-11

The word 'gifts' in the Greek is 'charisma' meaning 'undeserved favor and gifts of grace to show favor. The Spiritual Gifts of the Holy Spirit is the supernatural ability to carry out the work of Christ through His church. In addition, the church receives these gifts as God's unmerited favor upon us without anything we can do to earn it.

The Lord God has an excellent administrative system He uses to execute the administrations, operations and manifestations of the spiritual gifts through the Holy Spirit in the body of Christ. While there are different kinds of service, but the same Lord (1Corinthians 12:5, Ephesians 4:8), these gifts were unique. They are used in edification for the service and ministration of the church (1 Corinthians 12:5, NIV).

The gifts of the Father are motivational gifts which are inherent through Jesus Christ. Every believer has the ability to nurture and develop these seven gifts (Romans 12:6-8).

The gifts of the Son, Jesus Christ are administrative or ministry to the body of Christ. These gifts are to assist the body of Christ in the local church to grow and administration gifts (Ephesians 4:11; 1Corinthians 12; 28).

The gifts of the Holy Spirit are to implement the operation of the Spirit of God with power, and this is given to profit all, the body of Christ the church (1 Corinthians 12:7-11).

CHAPTER 8

FIVE-FOLD MINISTRIES GIFTS

The five-fold ministry is ordained by God.

Through the distinct roles of people that are true apostles, prophets, evangelists, pastors and teachers, their overall assignment is to equip the body of Christ at large, in doing the work of ministry; evangelizing the world, caring and healing the hurt as well as reaching the lost souls of this world for Jesus Christ.

With prophetic proliferation we will describe each ministry and encourage your charge to walk forward in it.

APOSTLE

The word Apostle is defined by the Greek word "apostolos," translated as "apostle" meaning one who is sent forth, a sent one. Jesus was the "sent one," an Apostle. He is called the Apostle and High Priest of our confession (Hebrew 3:1). Jesus as the Great Apostle did not come on His own; He was sent by His Father. He only did what He was sent to do. Those that received Him received the Father. As the Great Apostle, He became the blueprint of ministry for all other apostles.

There are two other usages of apostle; first the twelve apostles and the second referring to other individuals who are sent out to establish the government and order of God in churches as ambassadors of Jesus Christ.

In addition, apostles are sent out with the authority to establish churches on a solid foundation of God's word. They will strengthen existing churches in foundational doctrines and practical teaching from the Word. They will minister with boldness and authority and with revelatory knowledge through the Holy Spirit. They will function in all of the ministry giftings and operate in all of the gifts of the Holy Spirit. They will have a deep personal relationship with God and will have a father relationship to who he/ she ministers.

Signs, wonders and healing miracles will be continually manifested in their ministry. According to the word, 1 Thessalonians 2:6-8, Apostle's walks in humility, *"Nor did we seek glory from men, either from you or from others, when we might have made demands as apostles of Christ. But we were gentle among you, just as a nursing mother cherishes her own children. So, affectionately longing for you, we were well pleased to impart to you not only the gospel of God, but also our own lives, because you had become dear to us."*

Their ministry gifting is recognized and received as a relationship of the Holy Spirit to churches and other ministries. It will not be a relationship of human organization or denomination. From the spiritual relationship, the apostle will govern and bring necessary discipline, accountability, stability and protection from deception into the lives of believers, ministries and churches.

Further, the apostle will function closely with the ministry of the prophet in appointing and ordaining elders, confirming God's call on certain believer's lives and establishing them functioning in the ministry into which God has called them.

The apostle will impart and release believers into operation of the gifts of the Holy Spirit by the laying on of hands.

According to Acts 19:17-20, Apostles bring repentance, deliverance, revival and commitment among the people, "This became known both to all Jews and Greeks dwelling in Ephesus; and fear fell on them all, and the name of the Lord Jesus was magnified. And many who had believed came confessing and telling their deeds. Also many of those who had practiced magic brought their books together and burned them in the sight of all. And they counted up the value of them, and it totaled fifty thousand pieces of silver. So the word of the Lord grew mightily and prevailed."

As we have watched throughout the years, apostles frequently headed an apostolic team. This team consists of functioning fivefold ministry gifting. Each team member will be in close relationship with a church and accept and follow the spiritual leadership of the apostle. They labor together in doing front-line Kingdom building, establishing new churches, and in overseeing the rebuilding and ongoing development of existing churches.

PROPHETIC PROPHESY for APOSTLES

I caused you to be world changers and to think Big, with the authority to establish churches on a solid foundation of My Word! In addition, you will strengthen existing churches in foundational doctrine and practical teaching from My Word. You will minister with boldness and authority and with revelation knowledge by My Holy Spirit. You will have a deep personal relationship with Me and will be a spiritual father to many. I am charging you to walk in the spirit of excellence, humility, and in love. I am holding you accountable to govern and bring necessary discipline, accountability, stability, and protection from deception into the lives of believers, ministries and churches.

I have commissioned you to work with the other ministry gifts, especially with the prophets in order to bring repentance, deliverance, revival and commitment among My people. I charge you to impart and release believes into operation in the gifts of the Holy Spirit by the laying on of hands. Apostles, I have sent you out, but now is a new era of dispensation and I am bringing you in. I bring you into reorganizing my kingdom from within. Apostles, start from all ages which include my little children. As soon as they begin to talk start training them about my kingdom purpose.

Apostles arise within the Kingdom of God and demonstrate my glory and the awesomeness of my presence I placed upon you in this new era. In this new era you now realize its within my kingdom, my kingdom I am re-sculpturing, resetting and reorganizing for the purpose of strengthening my kingdom on the earth. Apostles I have placed an awesome anointing of my Holy Spirit presence within you for the task of reorganizing and rebuilding the body of Christ in this new era.

* *

PROPHET

Jesus was revealed as a prophet in the New Testament. His ministry as a prophet provides a blueprint for the ministry of prophets today. A prophet is one who speaks for God. A prophet has been given the distinctive ministry of representing God before men. Prophets will:

a. Give direction

b. Confirm guidance and vision

c. Give insight into the Word of God

d. Tell facts about people's lives

e. Rebuke

f. Judge

g. Correct

h. Warn

i. Reveal future events

Prophets will minister under a greater level of the prophetic anointing. There will be a greater detail and accuracy than the one who is simply operating in the gift of prophecy. The prophetic word from the prophet will contain revelation that goes beyond edification, exhortation and comfort. Prophets are a spokesman for God even as Aaron was a spokesman for Moses in Exodus 4:15, 16, "Now you shall speak to him and put the words in his mouth. And I will be with your mouth and with his mouth, and I will teach you what you shall do. So he shall be your spokesman to the people. And he himself shall be as mouth for you, and you shall be to him as God."

Prophets are never to speak his or her own thoughts or from his own wisdom. Prophets only speak when God is directing them as in 2 Peter 1:20, 21, "Know this first, that no prophecy of Scripture is of any private interpretation, for prophecy never came by the will of man, but holy men of God spoke as they were moved by the Holy Spirit."

There has been so much controversy over the words Prophet and Prophetess. However, the church needs to mature, souls are more important than a title of a person!

The word Prophet (male) /Prophetess (female) root comes from the Hebrew word Prophet. In God's eye, there is neither Jew nor Greek there is neither slave nor free, there is no male and female, for all are one in Christ Jesus (Galatians 3:28).

The above scripture refers to Jesus making no distinction between male & female. Therefore why should man make a difference in a prophet being a prophet male vs prophetess female when we are all one in the spirit in Christ Jesus?

Often a husband-wife team will operate in the same ministry gifting as did the prophet Isaiah and his wife, who was called a prophetess. Other husband-wife teams operate in different ministry gifting's such as a pastor and a teacher, or an apostle and a prophet. When this happens there is a great strength in the ministry. As a husband and wife who are one flesh, they are also one in the Spirit and will often flow and minister together with great strength in one ministry gifting.

True Prophets

True prophets of God, are shepherds. The prophets were given charge to go to the sheep fold and call to them a message from God (Isaiah 56:11and Ezekiel 34:2-8).

True prophets of God, are watchman, they watched the walls whose duty was to alert the people of the dangers approaching them (Isaiah

21-6-11, Ezekiel 3:17, 33-2). Sounding the alarm, the prophet warns the people. In addition they arouse the people to action.

Prosecutors in the Heavenly Court, prophets are God's spokesmen, presenting the case before God as judge in the Court of Heaven (1 Samuel 24:15, Psalms 43:1, Isaiah 34:8).

Prophets are a lion roaring, the voice is likened a lion's roar. Amos 3:7-8.

False Prophetess

False prophets prophesied lies; they gave the people what they wanted to hear. They have not stood in the council of God nor received words directly for the Lord. False prophets visions are drawn out of their own hearts (Jeremiah 14:14). In addition, some false prophets used magic according to Ezekiel 13:17-23, others appeared to use divination, soothsaying, witchcraft, necromancy, and sorcery, which were all forbidden arts and practices, according Deuteronomy 18:9-13.

Examples of a false prophet in the Old Testament and New Testament: Jeremiah 28 1:16, Hananiah prophesied a lie in ver. 11 saying thus said the LORD; Even so will I break the yoke of Nebuchadnezzar King of Babylon from the neck of all nations within the space of two full years. Ver. 15,16, Then said the prophet Jeremiah unto Hananiah the prophet, Hear now, Hananiah; The LORD hath not sent thee; but thou makest this people to trust in a lie. Therefore, thus said the LORD; Behold, I will cast thee from off the face of the earth: this year thou shalt die, because thou hast taught rebellion against the LORD.

Acts 13:6-10, And when they had gone through the isle unto Paphos, they found a certain sorcerer, a false prophet, a Jew, whose name was Barjesus: Which was with the deputy of the country, Sergius Paulus, a prudent man; who called for Barnabas and Saul, and desired to hear the word of God.

But Elymas the sorcerer withstood them, seeking to turn away the deputy from the faith. The Saul, filled with the Holy Ghost, set his eyes on him. And said, O full of all subtlety and all mischief, thou child of the devil, thou enemy of all righteousness, wilt thou not cease to pervert the right ways of the Lord?

If a prophet miss giving you an accurate word, or you feel that that word was not on point, that does not mean he/she is a false prophet. 1

Corinthians 13:9 NLT Now our knowledge is partial and incomplete, and even the gift of prophecy reveals only part of the whole picture! New International Version states For we know in part and we prophesy in part.

Judging a Prophecy

All prophets should allow and give an opportunity for all of their prophecies to be judged (1 Corinthians 14:29).

Beloved, do not believe every spirit, but test the spirits, whether they are of God; because many false prophets have gone out into the world (1 John 4:1).

Please remember, as humans we are fallible and subject to making mistakes. Just because a person gives a prophecy that's not right doesn't necessarily mean that they are a false prophet. When hearing a prophecy, judge it by asking questions like the following:

    a. Is the prophecy in harmony with the Word of God?

    b. Is the prophecy given in a good, non-condemning spirit? (Roman 8:34)

    c. Do his or her prophecies come to pass? (Deuteronomy 18:22)

    d. Does the person live a godly, Christ centered life? (Jeremiah 23:15,16)

    e. Does the Holy Spirit bear witness with your spirit regarding this prophecy? (1 John 2:20, 21)

    f. Has this been confirmed in the mouth of two or three witnesses? (2 Corinthians 13:1)

g. Does the fruit of the spirit manifest in their character? (Galatians 5:22)

Biblical manifestations of the call of the Prophets

a. Old testament Prophets

Most of the Old Testament is written by prophets, there referred to as major or minor prophets. Here is an example from Jeremiah 7:25, "Since the day that your fathers came out of the land of Egypt until this day, I have even sent to you all My servants the prophets, daily rising up early and sending them." These Prophets lives' were demonstrated through their prophesy to the nations like when Ezekiel who had to physically pack his bags for exile in the day time as the people watched (Ezekiel 12:3-6).

b. **Moses, a Pattern**

Moses was given a guideline for a prophetic ministry from which all future Old Testament prophets were judged. In the book of Deuteronomy, we read that Moses was like no other prophet. "But since then there has not arisen in Israel a prophet among you, I the LORD knew face to face," (Deuteronomy 34:10).

Visions and Dreams

(Genesis 15:1; Numbers 12:6; Job 4:13-16; Acts 7:30-32)

Visions and Dreams are a gift from God. God will reveal Himself and His plans to His prophets through visions. The message is received through some type of pictures. These pictures are received while awake by means of visions or while asleep through night dreams. Dreams give encouragement, direction, insight for intercession and revelation. In addition, a prophet may experience open visions, encounters, messages and being caught up in the Spirit.

Remember to develop that gift John 5:19:20, "Most assuredly, I say to you, the Son can do nothing of Himself, but what He sees the Father do, for whatever He does, the Son also does in like manner. For the Father loves the Son, and shows Him all things that He Himself does."

God's Word in Mouth (Deuteronomy 18:15:18)

God raised up Jesus and God has put His word in Jesus' mouth, which was the Kingdom is at Hand Mark 1:14. Jeremiah 1:9, Then the LORD reached out his hand and touched my mouth and said to me, "I have put my words in your mouth. Deuteronomy 18:15:18 .

The LORD your God will raise up for you a Prophet like me from your midst, from your brethren. Him you shall hear, according to all you desired of the LORD your God in Horeb in the day of the assembly, saying, "Let me not hear again the voice of the LORD my God, nor let me see this great fire anymore, lest I die." And the LORD said to me: "What they have spoken is good. I will raise up for them a Prophet like you from among their brethren, and will put My words in His mouth, and He shall speak to them all that I command Him.

Listening to a Prophet (Deuteronomy 18:19-20)

The prophets are a gift from God and they speak the word of God, and God tells us to listen to them in Jeremiah 26:5, 'And if you will not listen to my servants, the prophets, for I sent them again and again to warn you, but you would not listen to them, nor inclined your ear to hear.

Test of Prophecy (Deuteronomy 18: 21-22)

The Strong's Dictionary indicates 'Test' at 3985 to make proof of. Also, in 1381 to put to the test, prove, examine. We are to test (prove, examine) the spirits to see whether they are from God according to 1 John 4. In addition, the prophecy must be line up with the word of God.

If a prophet, or one who foretells by dreams, appears among you and announces to you a sign or wonder, and if the sign or wonder spoken of takes place, and the prophet says, "Let us follow other gods" (gods you have not known) "and let us worship them," you must not listen to the words of that prophet or dreamer. The LORD your God is testing you to find out whether you love him with all your heart and with all your soul.

Deuteronomy 13:1-3

Designations of the Prophets

a. Man of God

Prophets were men who were close to God and represented God in their daily life and ministry.

b. Seers & Prophets

Seer is another name for prophet as in 1 Samuel 9:9, "Before time in Israel, when a man went to enquire of God, thus he spoke, Come, and let us go to the seer; for he that is now called a seer." A seer is a prophet that sees vision, pictures or scenes in the mind's eye. A prophet also dreams with the natural eye; however not all prophets are Seers.

The prophets were the teachers, or interpreters of the law. They had given themselves to understand the spirit of the law rather than just the letter of the law. They interpreted the history of the nation in the light of the Word of the Lord. "Your first father sinned, and your mediators have transgressed against Me." Isaiah 43:27

c. **Prophets are Messengers** (Malachi 3:1; Amos 3:7)

   a. They testify that the Lord is coming to God's people like John the Baptist.

   b. Communicate too God's people before sin prophets Isaiah, Jeremiah, and Ezekiel.

   c. Prophets Isaiah, Jeremiah, and Ezekiel use writing to relay God's message in their messages along with Daniel are categorized as Major Prophets.

d. To announce judgment upon His people because they did not repent from sin

In addition, some prophet's life were the prophetic message itself. For example, Jonah's life was a prophetic message to Israel of future events. In chapter two Jonah's imprisonment in a great fish for three days and three nights and this symbolized Jesus death and resurrection of Christ verified this as prophetic of Himself (Matthew 12:40).

a. Prophets are Holy People of God according to the scriptures Deuteronomy 33:1, 1 Samuel 9:6-1 Kings 17:18-24 and 11Kings 4:7-9.

b. Prophets are full of the Spirit, their relationship comes from the Holy Spirit of God 1 Corinthians 14:37.

c. Prophets are anointed ones, they are commissioned and anointed to their office, called of God to his prophetic ministry. 1 Chronicles 16:22 and Psalms 105:15.

d. Prophets are servant due to their close relationship with the Lord. 11King9:7, 17:13, Jeremiah 7:25, Ezekiel 38:17, and Zechariah 1:6.

PROPHETIC PROPHESY FOR PROPHETS

I declare and decree that you direct, confirm, give insight into the word, tell the truth, rebuke, judge, correct, warn and prophesy. For you are My spokesman in the earth realm. I am saturating the prophets in My Spirit. I need you to continue to seek My face in this time. I will reveal My plans for

America, Nations, the Seven Mountains; Media, Government, Family, Arts and Entertainment, Economic, Religion, and Education. The winds of My Spirit are blowing through the land and My Churches. Everything that is not like Me will be blown away. My Glory will remain for you to see I am in the wind, which is My Spirit of Change, it is upon the land.

There has been such a put down for My prophets in this season. But now there is a new era, a new dispensation of time that has come upon you. Prophets shall arise with understanding and purpose to build and instruct My kingdom. Also, to demonstrate the words I have told you to do. For you see prophets, you are My fireballs and I have ignited you to throw those fireballs as you speak from the North, South, East and West in this new era of My kingdom. You will manifest the presence of the Lord like never before, because My seven Spirits are upon you. I will guide you, with the Spirit of the Lord, Spirit of knowledge, Spirit of wisdom, Spirit of understanding, Spirit of counsel, Spirit of might and the Spirit of the fear of the Lord like never before. For the kingdom of God is within and in this new season you will demonstrate my kingdom.

You will manifest My kingdom; speak My kingdom with that fire. The fire of the Most High God, the fire which burns; the fire that purifies, the fire that shows My kingdom glory and My presence. Even to the degree the smoke from the fireballs would create dark clouds that would hover over the earth like never before because of what I placed within you in this new season. You will demonstrate the presence of God like never before. It's the thick covering of the smoke from the fireballs that came from your mouths that My people will arise in the awareness of My manifest presence, My glory. This enhanced awareness will reveal My kingdom on the earth for the purpose of preparing My people for what is ahead of them.

* *

EVANGELIST

Evangelist can be interpreted as "Euaggelizo" in the Greek and refers to the ministry. It is defined to mean, announce good news or glad tidings. This word is referred to in the New Testament with regard to the ministry of Jesus as the Evangelist in Luke 4:18, "The Spirit of the Lord is upon Me, because He has anointed Me to preach the gospel to the poor. He has sent Me to heal the brokenhearted, to preach deliverance to the captives and recovery of sight to the blind, to set at liberty those who are oppressed."

In addition, according to the Word there were six things that were to characterize Jesus' ministry as evangelical:

  a. To preach the gospel to the poor
  b. To heal the brokenhearted
  c. To preach deliverance to the captives
  d. To recover sight to the blind
  e. To set at liberty those who are oppressed
  f. To preach the acceptable year of the Lord
  g. The "acceptable year of the Lord" was reference to the "Year Of Jubilee" and was the time for all bondage and debt to be released.

Luke explains and sees Jesus fulfilling His ministry as an Evangelist as prophesied by the Prophet Isaiah in the book of Luke chapter 4 verse 43, "But He said to them, "I must preach the kingdom of God to the other cities also, because for this purpose I have been sent."

And again in Luke 7:22, Then Jesus answered and said to them. "God and tell John the things you have seen and heard: That the blind see, the lame walk, the lepers are cleansed, the deaf hear, the dead are raised, the poor have the gospel preached to them."

Luke 8:1, Now it came to pass, afterward, that He went through every city and village, preaching and bringing the glad tidings of the kingdom of God. And the twelve were with Him.

And Luke 20:1 Now it happened on one of those days, as He taught the people in the temple and preached the gospel, that the chief priests and the scribes, together with the elders, confronted Him.

All believers are required to do the work of an evangelist even as Paul instructed Timothy in 2 Timothy 4:5, "But you be watchful in all things, endure afflictions, do the work of an evangelist, fulfill your ministry."

Every believer is to be His witness in accordance with Acts 1:8, "But you shall receive power when the Holy Spirit has come upon you; and shall be witnesses to Me in Jerusalem, and in all Judea and Samaria, and to the end of the earth."

All believers are to evangelize; the evangelist has an anointing for evangelism and will therefore be more skilled in this area of ministry. Looking at Philip's life in the New Testament; Acts 21:8, we can learn that he was:

a. **Committed**

Philip was committed to the local church in Jerusalem. Later in Caesarea, this became his home.

b. **Good reputation**

Philip had proven himself to the leadership of his home church as a man of character and integrity.

c. **Full of Spirit**

He was continuously full of the Holy Spirit.

d. **Proven Wisdom**

He was a man proven in wisdom.

e. **Servant's Heart**

Philip had a servant's, heart. His heart
was full of compassion and he responded
to the needs of those in need. He walks
as a humble man, willing to serve others.

f. Proven Service

Philip proves himself as a deacon before
he became an evangelist.

g. Submitted to Authority

Philip submitted himself first to the
authority of the elders which helped him
to learn authority.

h. Recommended by Elders

Philip had the spiritual support of the
elders at his local church.

Philip recognized the limitations of his own
ministry; he knew that he did not have to do
everything himself. He worked with others, which

demonstrated a willingness to work with other ministries in service to the Kingdom.

So many times the body of Christ does not realize that we need each other working together in unity. Let's look at our hand which symbolizes the fivefold ministry gifts. The apostle is the thumb working with all other fingers. The prophet is the pointer-finger saying, "thus saith the Lord," and the longest outreach is the evangelist. The wedding ring finger is the pastor symbolizing the special love relationship between himself and the people. The little finger is the teacher who works closely with the pastor and is much needed for balance. Just as all five fingers are needed for a complete, functioning hand, all ministries are needed for the complete building up of the saints.

The evangelist preaches one main message. It is the gospel of Jesus Christ. Everywhere Philip went as an evangelist, he proclaimed Jesus Christ (Acts 8:5). Moreover, a strong part of the message of an evangelist is to those who receive Jesus in water (baptism) as a seal and a testimony of their faith in Jesus Christ.

In addition, the new believers need to be baptized in the Holy Spirit as it states in Acts 8:14-17, "Now when the apostles who were at Jerusalem heard that Samaria had received the word of God, they sent Peter and John to them, who when they had come down, prayed for them that they might receive the Holy Spirit. For as yet He had fallen upon none of them. They had only been baptized in the name of the Lord Jesus. They laid hands on them, and they received the Holy Spirit. This baptism gives the new believer the power to be witnesses and to keep taking the gospel to others who had not yet heard."

The power this scripture speaks of is to fulfill the great commission just as in Mark 16:15-18, "And He said to them, 'Go into all the world and preach the gospel to every creature. He who believes and is baptized will be saved, but he who does not believe will be condemned. And these signs will follow those who believe: In My name they will cast out demons; they will speak with new tongues; they will take up serpents; and if they drink anything deadly, it will by no means hurt them; they will lay hands on the sick, and they will recover.'"

The only truly effective evangelism is miracle evangelism. The traditional and religious methods and techniques without the Holy Spirit will not work. God will confirm His Word with signs and wonders. Too often the church has a form of godliness, but have denied its power (2 Timothy 3:5).

PROPHETIC PROPHESY FOR EVANGELIST

I declare and decree that evangelists arise and be reset. Let the fear of the Lord come upon every soul. Let many wonders and signs be done through them. Let the Lord add to His church daily. Let the multitudes of men, women, and children come from the North, South, East and West of our city, states, and nation to accept the Lord, and fulfill the great commission. You will teach, preach and prophesy in my anointing to break the chains of the enemy so that My people will come out of their prison cells. I declare and decree that you preach the gospel to the poor, heal the brokenhearted, preach deliverance to the captives, recover sight to the blind, set at liberty those who are oppressed and preach the acceptable year of the Lord.

Evangelist, go and make disciples of my kingdom and stop compromising. No longer compromise with what you desire for yourself. It's not about you but about my kingdom. Make disciples of my kingdom in this new dispensation, for what you see, you must become built up spiritually. There is no time to take it easy, no time to lay by the wayside but to arise and go forward and make disciples of my kingdom like never before. Disciples, Disciples for my kingdom is my true purpose of the kingdom of God. The trueness is God's kingdom there is no other true kingdom but My Kingdom. In this new era, evangelist, my word

74

has already commanded you to make disciples for the kingdom of God.

* *

Pastor/Bishop

Pastor translated in the Greek as in Ephesians 4:11 is "poimen," meaning shepherd, one who tends herds or flocks, guides, as well as feed the flock, an overseer (Acts 20:28).

The Greek word for overseer is "episkopos." This can also be translated to "bishop." Whenever you see the word, it means one who feeds the sheep. It is simply a reference to a pastor or a shepherd. A bishop in a scriptural context is a function in the local church, not one who has authority over a group of local churches as does an apostle.

Pastors (Shepherd's) need to care for their sheep and flock; which refers to God's people. In this way, God's people:

a. **Need special care.**

Sheep need special care. They are the most dependent of all of God's creatures (Genesis 4:2).

b. **Need to be Fed.**

Sheep need to be fed as in 1 Samuel 17: 15, 20, "But David occasionally went and returned from Saul to feed his father's sheep at Bethlehem. So David rose early in the morning, left the sheep with a keeper and took the things and went as Jesse had commanded him. And he came to the camp as the army was going out to the fight and shouting for the battle."

c. **Get lost easily**

Sheep as in God's people, tend to wander from flock to flock just like believer's wander from church to church. Some sheep are vulnerable due to a Shepherd being wolves in sheep's clothes. God will use a good shepherd to seek them out so that they may be delivered (Ezekiel 34:12).

d. **Need protection**

Sheep, by themselves, are open prey to all kinds of wild animals. Wild animals can represent false prophets; people in the five-fold ministry teaching another Jesus and gospel. Sheep need protection from false prophets (Matthew 7:15).

e. Are Valuable

Sheep are so valuable that Jesus Christ laid down his life for His sheep. How precious is that?

f. Need shepherd to survive

Psalms 23 is an excellent example of the great Shepherd and why the sheep / believers need Him to survive.

As in John 10:1-3, Jesus is our shepherd, "Most assuredly, I say to you, he who does not enter the sheepfold by the door, but climbs up some other way, the same is a thief and a robber. But he who enters by the door is the shepherd of the sheep. To him, the doorkeeper opens, and the sheep hear his voice, and he calls his own sheep by name and leads them out."

A sheepfold was a wall surrounding an open area from which the sheep came and went. This sheepfold symbolizes how Jesus is the gate. He is the gate and the only man who enters by the gate or is called by God, can be a true shepherd to the sheep.

John 10:4-5 And when he brings out his own sheep, he goes before them; and the sheep follow him, for they know his voice. Yet they will by no means follow a stranger but will flee from him, for they do not know the voice of strangers.

The shepherds should operate in all the gifts of the Holy Spirit. However, the revelation gifts are especially important to the ministry of the shepherd. God will warn the shepherd of danger by the operation of the gift of the distinguishing between spirits. There is a great protection for the church and a greater effectiveness in a pastor/ shepherd's ministry as they are led by the Holy Spirit, moment by moment!

PROPHETIC PROPHESY FOR PASTOR/SHEPHERD

Pastors I release My anointing of grace upon you to continue to care for my sheep. But even as you've been caring for the sheep in times past, you've been weary in well doing. I called you not to faint nor get weary in well doing. Truly you shall reap what you have sowed if you faint not. Your labor of love has not been forgotten nor is it in vain. I am the good shepherd who has set the standards for you with the laying down of My life for the advancement of My kingdom. My Holy Spirit is within you to operate in a more excellent way. I have opened up the revelatory realm to you by My Spirit to help you to discern the differences between what is from Me and what is not. I loose My strength, peace, and joy on you now to do the greater work.

Pastors my sheep are crying. My sheep are crying, stop being partial to my sheep. There is neither Jew nor Greek, male nor female, slave or free so stop being partial and showing favoritism to my sheep; my sheep are crying.

Pastors rise up in this new era. I will move mountains on behalf of my sheep when I hear the cries of my sheep. I am judging my pastors. Pastors stop being partial to my congregations and preach my full gospel. Pastors minister my gospel and shepherd my people. They need your caring, they need your cleansing, they need your watering, they need your nurturing and they need your pastoring in this new season. Be the pastors I called you to be, within my kingdom stop being partial to my sheep.

* *

TEACHER

A teacher is one who instructs and by their teachings causes others to learn. Their teachings involve demonstration and explanation of Scripture and instruction in doctrine to others. The disciples went forward teaching and preaching the word of God, everywhere after Jesus Christ resurrection. The gospel was confirmed after teaching and preaching with signs and wonders following (Mark 16:19-20). This was the pattern Jesus established; teach and preach results were signs and wonders of the supernatural.

Jesus is our prime example of the Teacher. (Ephesians 4:11). The teaching ministry holds an important place in the New Testament. The teacher is the only one mention by name in all three list of the ministry gifting's given in scripture.

The purpose of teaching is necessary for unity, growth, maturity and to equip believers for service. Furthermore, maturity manifests when the believers understand their vision, identity, purpose, and destiny. That includes the believer studying the word, mediating on the word, speaking and living the word (Habakkuk 2:2,4; Ephesians 4:15).

There are two Hebrew words used for teacher in the Old Testament which reveal the nature of the teacher's ministry:

a. Inform

"Yarah" means to flow as water (as rain) to point out (as with the finger). It has been translated as: direct, inform,

instruct, lay, shoot, show, teach through
and rain.

Now therefore, go, and I will be with
your mouth and teach you what you
shall say (Exodus 4:12,15).

b. Diligently Instruct

"Lamad" means to goad, or by
implication, to teach by the incentive of
the rod. It has been translated as:
diligently instruct, learn, skillful, teach,
teacher or teaching.

There are six Greek words used for a teacher
found in the New Testament. Each of the words
came from the same root word as the two words;
inform and instruct:

a. To instruct

"Didasko" means to learn or to teach. It is translated teach.

b. Instructive

"Didaktikos' means instructive. It is translated apt to teach.

c. Instructed of

"Didaktos" means instructed of, convicted by teaching and is translated taught

d. Instruction (Noun)

"Dikaskalia" means instruction, the function or the information. It is translated doctrine, learning, and teaching.

e. An Instructor

"Dikaskolos" means an instructor and it's translated:

1. 14 times referred to as Doctor

2. 47 times referred to as Master

3. 10 times referred to as Teacher

4. 67 times referred to as Scribe

f. Instruction (Verb)

"Didache" means instruction, the act of instruction. It is translated "doctrine, has been taught."

A teacher is, therefore, one who instructs, and by teaching causes others to learn. It involves exposition, explanation, and instruction of doctrine to others. The teacher who is a part of the fivefold ministry has been chosen by God to instruct others.

Jesus was a Teacher wherever He went. He spent much of His time teaching the multitudes (Matthew 9:35). When Jesus taught, he taught with authority according to Matthew 7:28, 29, "And so it was, when Jesus had ended these sayings, that the people were astonished at His teaching, for He taught them as one having authority, and not as the scribes."

Jesus' success was due to the fact that He taught only what He received from His Father and that He taught in the anointing and power of the Holy Spirit. John 8:28, "Then Jesus said to them, "When you lift up the Son of Man, then you will know that I am He and that I do nothing of Myself; but as My Father taught Me, I speak these things."

How did Jesus teach?

   a. **Used illustrations** (Matthew 9:16)
   b. **Told Parables** (Mark 4:34)
   c. **Started where people were** (John 4:10, 15, 25, 26)
   d. **Used miracles to prove His message** (Luke 5:17)
   e. **Used teaching to bring about unity** (John 17:21, 1 Corinthians 3:5-11)
   f. **Carried the mark of a teacher**

Characteristics of a biblical teacher that is willing to yield to the Holy Spirit studies the bible rightly dividing the word of truth.

Also, teachers communicate, they guide, and they are pliable. They disciple and display the characteristics of Christ. They are an instructor to patience. We believe the results of every good teacher are to become like the teacher, knowing what is true and what is false. Jesus was the truth and so much more. He said "I am the way the truth and the life. No man comes to the Father except through me," (John 14:6).

Jesus Christ is the believer's Master Teacher and He has taught them the above scripture in John. To obtain eternal life one must go through Christ. When a teacher can teach this, then they will be like the Master Teacher, Jesus Christ.

GIFTS WITHIN THE GIFT

We cannot help but warn you of the importance of being a teacher as in James 3:1-2 which warns us that a teacher should not want to become teachers due to them being judged with a greater strictness. A false teacher does exist and would be judged with severe punishment.

Special Anointing

There is a special anointing upon teachers. *But ye have an anointing from the Holy One, and you know all things* (1 John 2:20, 27)

The anointing which you have received from Him abides in you. As the same anointing teaches you concerning all things, in all truth, you will abide in Him and He in the words you teach.

Gentle Spirit

Teachers must have a gentle spirit.

In, 1 Peter 3:4, Peter's instruction was to the women; however, God requires both male & female to demonstrate a gentle and quiet spirit. It's the inside person that is valuable to God more than the outside. He mentions out of the abundance of the mouth the heart speaks. Therefore teachers must be careful to walk in a gentle spirit.

Dependent on Holy Spirit

Teachers must be dependent upon the Holy Spirit. Jesus Christ did nothing without the Holy Spirit; He is the Spirit of Christ and the Holy Spirit is manifested as the seven Spirits of God. Jesus Christ had informed his disciples that, He would be leaving but He would ask the Father to send them another Counselor, which is the Spirit of Truth John 14:16-17.

The Greek work for "Counselor; in the above scripture, is *'parakletos'* means one called to the side of another that would counsel, support the needs of those that want it. We know Paraclete is God's Holy Spirit; the third person in the Trinity. He is a person and His purpose is to dwell within the believers, aiding the believer in obtaining revelation from the word of truth. Also, he brings to the believer's remembrance the things that Jesus Christ has taught them. He is the Gift that gives out the gifts. Also, the gifts are demonstrated through Him with power. The Holy Spirit is the mighty power source.

Teaches with Authority

Teachers must teach with authority.

The Bible was created with authority as one of its foundations; the body of Christ is an organization that manifests this authority with its founder Jesus Christ. In Matthew 7:28, 29 Jesus Christ taught with authority and how much his body should teach with authority.

And so it was, when Jesus had ended these sayings, that the people were astonished at His teaching, for He taught them as one having authority, and not as the scribes.

Teaches multiplication

Jesus taught multiplication as a biblical principle in the Bible. In God's economy, his blessings turns into multiplication.

There are at least two biblical examples of this. One occurs in 2 Kings 4: 1-7 where God supernaturally multiplied the widow's oil, note oil in earlier chapters indicates a symbol of the Holy

Spirit. The other when occurs when Jesus multiplied the loaves of bread and the fishes in Luke 9:16. In the end, Jesus blessed and broke the loaves of bread (and fish) giving them to the disciples to set before the multitude.

Jesus multiplication principle pertaining to the loaves of bread and fishes were that:

a. He "Blessed" them; executed resources by faith,

b. He "Broke" them; allowed God to bless it,

c. He "Gave" them; allowed God to give it back and then,

d. He discipled; "Gave" it to the multitude so you can Give it away also.

Openness

Openness from a teacher relies totally on the Holy Spirit. The Holy Spirit will instruct the teacher's in everything (John 14:26), walking and living in the Spirit is a necessity for understanding (2 Corinthian 3:15-17) and teaching God's word. Teachers realize they have no power to change anyone's heart, but it's through the Holy Spirit that gives them at power to transform lives all because of the grace of God.

Student of the Word

A student of God's word is a believer who studies and meditates on the word of God. A Christian student's lifelong study will never end.

Its benefits are in Psalms 1, 'meditate day and night, they are like a tree planted by streams of water, which will yields it fruit in season and whose leaf does not wither. Whatever the student does that coincides with the word of God shall prosper. Also, being a student of the word is to learn to discern the three voices in this world, God's, man and Satan due to growing in the spirit.

Always teaches others

It is an obligation for teachers to teach others regardless of the different levels. One just must be apt to teach meaning able to teach. Paul in his farewell comments to the Elders at Ephesian in Acts 20:20, did not hesitate to teach from house to house.

Accuracy

It is imperative that a minister/ teacher teach with accuracy. In Acts 18:25 Apollos an educated man, spoke with great intensity, who was knowledgeable about Jesus through John the Baptist teaching. However, in verse 26, Priscilla and Aquila heard him they invited him to their home and explained to him a more excellent way which was more accurate. All believers should manifest the tenacity to push forward and learn a more excellent way pertaining to the gospel of Jesus Christ. This includes being baptized in Holy Spirit and speaking in tongues as a more excellent way. This also includes learning and demonstrating the ministry of deliverance. In addition, allowing the Holy Spirit to work through you in demonstrating signs and wonders within the body of Christ who need healing is a more excellent way. Finally giving people prophetic words in the market place or in their environment is also a more excellent way.

Exemplary Life

The believer knows and understands why Jesus Christ lived an exemplary life. For example, look at Peter. Peter went through a metamorphose;

from a loud grandstanding man to a quiet man of strength and grace. If Jesus Christ has done that to Peter, how much more can He do for us? Therefore there is hope for the believer (1Peter 2:1-2, 3).

Teaches to Change Lives

Biblical teaching can change lives to manifest and renew the heart/mind and the ability to discern good and evil (Hebrews 5:14). Biblical teaching change believer's lives on listening and obeying the voice of God. Living a life of worship (Romans 12; 1), they are mature in passing on biblical knowledge to the generation and the future generation.

Financial Support

A teacher should be supported financially by those that they are teaching. Galatians 6:6 Let him who is taught the word share in all good things with him who teaches.

Methods of teachings

Different teaching methods are examples of everyday life like Joseph a son of Jacob. Symbols of animals are used as teaching methods like the dove that represented the Holy Spirit and the Lion of the tribe of Judah (Revelations 5:5). Also, let us not forget Jesus Christ taught in parable, demonstration, and storytelling. Declaration, is another method for teaching.

By Declaration

The biblical declaration is words that are spoken by the believer, for the purpose of proclaiming the word of God true to them. In the beginning, God declared "everything into existence and it was so." In Isa 42:8-9, NET Bible, I am the Lord! That is my name! I will not share my glory with anyone else, or the praise due me with idols. V. 9 Look, my earlier predictive oracles have come to pass; now I announce new events. Before they begin to occur, I reveal them to you.

Declaration fortifies God makes the dead alive and summons the things that do not yet exist as though they already do (Romans 4:17, NET). For example in 2 Timothy 3:10 it says, "But you have carefully followed my doctrine, manner of life, purpose, faith, long-suffering, love, perseverance."

John 13:12-15 So when He had washed their feet, taken His garments, and sat down again, He said to them, "Do you know what I have done to you? You call me Teacher and Lord, and you say well, for so I am. If I then, your Lord and Teacher, have washed your feet, you also ought to wash one another's feet. For I have given you an example that you should do as I have done to you."

What to Watch for

The Scripture below informs believers to watch for the works of the flesh.

Galatians 5:19-21 and those that are not teaching sound doctrine of Jesus Christ. Also, Colossians 2:8 NET, Be careful not to allow anyone to captivate you through an empty, deceitful philosophy that is according to human traditions and the elemental spirits of the world, and not according to Christ.

1 Timothy 6:3-5 If anyone teaches otherwise and does not consent to wholesome words, even the words of our Lord Jesus Christ, and to the doctrine which is according to godliness, he is proud,

knowing nothing, but is obsessed with disputes and arguments over words, from which come envy, strife, reviling, evil suspicions, useless wrangling of men of corrupt minds and destitute of the truth, who suppose that godliness is a means of gain. From such withdraw yourself.

False Doctrine

In Christianity, a true Biblical doctrine is that there is only one God in all existence (Isaiah 43:10, 44:6, 8). A false doctrine is that there is more than one God in all existence. In Christianity Jesus Christ is the Son of God, our Savior and Messiah which means anointed one. He is Christ that manifests three offices Prophet, Priest, and King. In false doctrine implies Jesus Christ is not the Son of God and He is not a Savior.

2 Peter 2:1 But there were also false prophets among the people, even as there will be false teachers among you, who will secretly bring in destructive heresies, even denying the Lord who bought them, and bring on themselves swift destruction.

2 Timothy 4:3 For the time will come when they will not endure sound doctrine, but according to their own desires, because they have itching ears, they will heap up for themselves teachers.

Traditions of Men

Traditions of man manifest into modern Christianity are Easter, Halloween, St. Valentine's Day, St. Patrick's Day, and Christmas. Constantine plays an important part in deciding when Jesus' birth would be celebrated through the centuries.

Constantine incorporated pagan holidays into Christianity to satisfy his pagan community. Also, to unify his empire, or to make converting to Christianity not difficult, Constantine sought to intermingle Christian and pagan traditions. During that time, there were two prominent pagan winter festivals that were celebrated. The first, starting on December 17 and lasting seven days honored Saturn, the Roman god of agriculture. The second, starting on December 25 and lasting through January 1, commemorated the birth of Mithras, the Persian god of light. We suggest that you research on your own and find out the origin of each modern day Christian holiday. To aid you in your research, read the 1611 original language Bible. A lot of the newer translation Bibles are using functional equivalence principles or otherwise paraphrase and diminish their meaning. One can obtain a free PDF copy of the 1611 Bible online by Googling it.

Judge, with the help of the Holy Spirit, to retain it or release it. Mark 7:8, NET, "Having no regard for the command of God, you hold fast to human tradition."

Judge by Word

As a teacher, what you say is important; you will be judged by the words you use to teach in accordance with the word of God.

Judge by Motivation

God judges the hearts of men to see if their motives are good, evil or selfish and judge them accordingly. Motivation is the force that is behind our behaviors, and it gives the reason for people's actions, desires, and needs (Jeremiah 17:10).

The dictionary meaning of the word 'judge' means to discern, to distinguish, to form an opinion, to compare facts or ideas, and to perceive agreement or disagreement, and thus to distinguish truth from falsehood.

This is what the Bible mentions about judging:

"The mouth of the righteous speaketh wisdom, and his tongue talketh of judgment." (Psalms 37:30)

"With my lips have I declared all the judgments of thy mouth." (Psalms 119:13)
"Open thy mouth, judge righteously, and plead the cause of the poor and needy." (Proverbs 31:9)

"Jesus commended Simon, "Thou hast rightly judged." (Luke 7:43)

"Now, thou son of man, wilt thou judge, wilt thou judge the bloody city? yea, thou shalt show her all her abominations." (Ezekiel 22:2)

"But he that is spiritual judgeth all things, yet he himself is judged of no man." (1 Corinthians 2:15)

"Do ye not know that the saints shall judge the world? and if the world shall be judged by you, are ye unworthy to judge the smallest matters?" (1 Corinthians 6:2)
"Know ye not that we shall judge angels? How much more things that pertain to this life?" (1 Corinthians 6:3)

Judge Relationship

Relationship with God

You judge your relationship with God is it a set of rules, regulation, and obligations or a relationship that understands you are loved by God as his children with an intimate relationship with him. We consider ourselves having a personal relationship with God through His Son Jesus Christ; who gave His life for us. It's God's liquid love that permeates our souls in obedience to His words, which increase a passion within us. Hebrews 4:16. Therefore let us confidently approach the throne of grace to receive mercy and find grace whenever we need help.

Relationship with Christians

Believers do not be ignorant of Satan devices, you are fruit inspectors (Galatians 5:22-23).

PROPHETIC PROPHESY FOR TEACHERS

My beloved teachers, you are the ones who are close to my heart. I have given you this gift through the Holy Spirit. You have My given ability to explain My Word, to clearly instruct and communicate knowledge, specifically the doctrine of faith and truths of the Bible. Some of My sheep have gone astray or are lost in the cares of this world, through false teaching. My Spirit within you will reveal all truth, which will set my people free from ignorance! How
can they learn without you? My teachers for I have appointed and anointed you to teach the unadulterated truth of My Word.

Teachers the words you teach from, My Word, is like a vehicle for communication, therefore it is very important to guard the heart. I strengthen you this day, in the power of Might and My Word. So to continue to seek me for fresh wisdom, revelation, and creativity to teach! Say no to ungodliness and worldly passions, and live self-control, upright godly lives in this present age!

Teachers, in this new dispensation there has truly been a paradigm shift. No longer will the old do. You are to teach my unadulterated word of God with truth, the full gospel of Jesus Christ, in this new season.

Just like Nehemiah. He had the people have a sword in one hand and a brick in the another hand building the walls. Teachers your sword is the word of God, unadulterated word of God. The brick is the divine teaching, the divine purpose and the divine attributes as you lay each brick you are laying what

I have placed within my kingdom to demonstrate my power. You will rise up and say no more compromising my kingdom principles. Each brick would have a demonstration of my kingdom, my principles, my glory and my gospel on them, not to compromise. From your teaching the unadulterated word of God, you will build strong bricks that are divinely made. Those brick will build strong walls within my kingdom so my people would know there is no compromising, no compromising in this new season. In this new era, the purpose is to build the walls without compromising my gospel.

So teach and demonstrate my gospel without compromising with signs, wonders, and miracles in this new season.

Nine Ministries of Believers Gifts
a. Prophesying

This means God speaks to and through them to others for the edification, exhortation, and comfort of God's people (1Corinthians 14:3).

b. Deacon or Helps

For the service of the ministry, to give assistance to others in the body of Christ so the five-fold ministry can focus on the ministry. This can include plethora duties from cleaning to visiting the sick and elderly, deacon duties, etc... (1 Corinthian 12:28).

c. Teaching

Instructing others in the Bible godly, logical and systematic way. As the teacher communicates the word of God in a way the student can grow and understand it (Romans 12:7; 1 Corinthians 12:28).

d. Exhortation

To exhort is to give encouragement, comfort, consolation, counsel and assist them to mature in Christ (Romans 12:8). The pastor, counseling leader, all those that are in the church can participate in exhortation.

e. Giving

Giving means to encouragement, comfort, consolation, counsel and assist them to mature in Christ (Romans 12:8). The pastor, counseling leader, all those that are in the church can participate in exhortation.

f. Administration

To aid/direct the body of Christ to accomplish the goals God have given them, planning, organizing and supervising (1Corinthians 12:28).

g. Mercy

Mercy is evident when believers' become sensitive toward others that are suffering, hurting physically, physically, and psychologically. Feeling true sympathy speaking words of compassion from the heart manifesting the God kind of love in helping them in their time of need (Romans 12; 8).

h. Healing

Healing is when the Holy Spirit working through believers' in healing people physically, emotionally, psychologically and spiritually (1Corinthians 12:9, 28, 30).

i. Tongues and Interpretation

Tongues to speak in an unknown language, so the unbelievers' can hear God's message in their own language for the edified of the body of Christ (1 Corinthians 12:10; 14:27, 28).

CHAPTER 9

DIVERSITIES OF OPERATION

We have different gifts, according to the grace given
to each of us. (Romans 12:6). God's manifest
versatility in His modes of operation is not set in
stone. Let's observe the life of individuals' who the
spiritual gifts of the Holy Spirit manifest with their
techniques of action.

Moses & Elijah

Moses and Elijah were prophets in the Old
Testament, they were used mightily. God's Spirit
came upon them demonstrating awesome signs,
wonders and miracles. However, their techniques of
action were different; Moses technique was to use a
rod for working miracles (Exodus 4:2, 20; 7:9).

Elijah's technique was using his mantle (2 Kings 2:8, 13-14).

Peter & Paul

Peter and Paul were apostles whom God's Holy Spirit dwelled within. They manifested the kingdom of God with powerful signs and wonders. However, their techniques of action were different. Peter's action of healing and miracles came through his shadow (Acts 5:15). But Paul's technique for uncommon miracles came through his hands (Acts 19:11-12).

Have you noticed the same ministry gifts with a different administration that each individual highlighted demonstrates? God love's uniqueness!

CHAPTER 10

DIFFERENCES OF GIFTS

When the one Gift, the Holy Spirit came from Abba Father, He dispersed nine gifts to the believer. And the only requirement to receive these gifts is for the believer to be baptized in the Holy Spirit (Acts 2:38).

Under that baptism you can receive the following gifts:

1. Gift of the word of wisdom

2. Gift of the word of knowledge

3. Gift of faith

4. Gifts of healings

5. Gift of working of miracles

6. Gift of prophecy

7. Gift of discerning of spirits

8. Gift of different kinds of tongues

9. Gift of Interpretation of tongues.

The gifts of the Holy Spirit are tripartite manifest in three different categories. God loves to operate in threes like the Triune God which is Father, Son, and Holy Spirit. The gifts correlate with the understanding the Heavenly Father, the manager who is papa, that establishes the gifts. Further, the Son, represents being the lover in operation of these gifts, the healer who loves the Father and God's people. The Holy Spirit then represents the worker of the gifts. He helps the body of Christ operate in the gifts and He carries out the plans of God.

1. Gifts of Revelation (reveal something)

In revealing about the Holy Spirit and His works, the Lord Jesus said, "the Spirit of truth, whom the world cannot receive because it neither sees Him nor knows him; but you know Him, for He dwells with you and will be in you. But the Helper, the Holy Spirit, whom the Father will send in My name, He will teach you all things and bring to your remembrance all things that I said to you," (John 14: 17, 26).

In the scriptures above, Jesus reveals the foundation of which the gifts of revelation work.

The gift of revelation enables us as believers to become aware of the Spiritual realm and to acknowledge the things in the past, present and the future. The tripartite gifts are in this category; Revelation, Power and Communication; each category having tripartite with them.

Group 1 Revelation Gifts

Word of Wisdom:

The "word" in Greek is logos meaning a small word. The word of wisdom has a supernatural technique to ascertain the divine means for accomplishing God's will in any situation. The divine means are from the Holy Spirit to give men revelation of future events about the earth, humanity and the universe. In addition to the plans, purposes, the mind of God, and revelation of God Himself. Word of wisdom manifests life changing illumination in one's personal life. Moreover, it's not a natural ability. Nor can you earn it. It is only given by the Holy Spirit.

This word of wisdom can be used interactively with two other revelation gifts; word of knowledge and discernment. Remember 'word' implied in the Greek; logos means a small world. This gift represents part of a whole like a splash of water. A splash represents a small amount of water, not the full capacity.

Spirit of Wisdom

In comparison to the word of wisdom, the spirit of wisdom is like emerging oneself in the ocean; it is vast. It's supernatural perspective to ascertain the divine means for accomplishing God's will in any situation as the Holy Spirit administers in each believer. It enlightens our spiritual understanding and knowledge of the word of God. It also enables us to know what to do and when to do it in every situation. The spirit of wisdom is the maximum manifestation of God's abilities in its full potential. It also reveals the wisdom of God's secrets of things in heaven and on earth.

Word of Knowledge

A word of knowledge manifests as a belief, impression or just a knowing that comes to you in the likeness of a mental picture, a dream, a vision or a scripture that quickens you. The nature of it is supernatural insight given by the Holy Spirit for an understanding of a specific circumstance, situation or any problem.

Group 2 Power Gifts

Power Gifts (That do something)

When the Helper comes, whom I will send to you from the Father, the Spirit of truth who goes forth from the Father, He will bear witness concerning Me.

(John 15:26 Berean Literal Bible).

The above scripture inform us of the power gifts before Jesus Christ ascended into heaven. Here He communicates to his disciples that they would be His witnesses after they received power from the Holy Spirit (Luke 24:48-49; Acts 1:8).

Power gifts give us legal power to perform signs, wonders, healings, and miracles through the Holy Spirit like the Lord Jesus (John 14:12). These tripartite gifts categories are listed below.

Faith Gift

The gift of faith function is to perform something impossible by ordinary people with the help of the Holy Spirit; without doubt or unbelief. In this gift, the believer has supernatural ability to obtain special faith in believing God for receiving miracles.

The faith gift engages the operation of the invisible and boundless resources of heaven which allow the Holy Spirit to work through you and for you. This gift is also called mountain moving faith (Mark 11:22, 23; 1 Corinthians 13:2).

The Faith gift is powerful as the Lord Jesus define its measurement which is "nothing will be impossible" when this gift is in full operation (Matthew 17:20). When this gift is in manifestation, it refuses to take a no for an answer. This gift knows God is the God of possibilities.

Healing Gift

The gift of healing is the supernatural ability imparted by the Holy Spirit to a believer to manifest healing miracles without any doctors.

The core principle is to know that the healing gift is to know it is God's complete will to heal sicknesses (Isaiah 53:5; Matthew 8:16, 17; 1 Peter 2:24; 3 John 2). Our souls must become saturated with this fundamental which would close the door for doubt and the type of unbelief that would paralyze our faith to believe.

Working of Miracles

The gift of the working of miracles is the supernatural or natural gift with accurate timing, to bring glory to God. This gift is endowed and imparted by God's Holy Spirit to work a miracle by which natural laws are altered, suspended or controlled. Working of miracles and operations of its power used to energize powerful works, can intervene and counteract earthly and evil forces. Miracles come from the Greek word 'dunams' which mean 'power and might that multiplies itself.

Furthermore, this gift does correlate with power, the gift of faith and the gift of healing to have victory and authority over Satan's sickness and sin.

Group 3 Communication / Inspiration Gifts
Communication Gifts (That say something)
Prophecy

When a believer accepts Jesus Christ into their life His DNA flows through him/her, which gives them the ability/authority to prophesy (Numbers 11:25-26; Acts 19:6). This means God speaks to and through them to others for the edification (build up), exhortation (admonition or encouragement) and comfort of God's people (1Corinthians 14:3).

The Testimony of Jesus is the Spirit of prophecy (Rev 19:10). The purpose of this scripture is one thing but the principle behind it is another. I once heard a Pastor explain the principle of

'Testimony of Jesus is the Spirit of prophecy;' which is any spoken or written record of what Jesus has done. This is the spirit of prophecy, speaking forth the mind and counsel of God and foretelling the future. The gift of Prophecy has an anointing to change lives in the now. Simply put, a Testimony has the power to adjust the way things are now. There is revelation in the 'now' (Hebrews 11:1).

The gift of prophecy can function in the life of any believer. However, when the gift of prophecy is operating through a believer other than a prophet, or one of the ministry giftings, it will normally contain revelation beyond that for which the gift of prophecy is specifically given. The purpose of this is for strengthening, encouragement, and comfort of God's people.

Different Kinds of Tongues

Different kinds of tongues and interpretation of tongues coincide together to work in concordance with the blessing of building up the body of Christ. Further, both manifest as one. It's a necessity that they operate together because they are intertwined together. However, the gift of different kinds of tongues can operate and manifest individually when it's needed.

This gift is not the familiar gift of speaking in tongues when a person is baptized with the Holy Spirit; which is one of the evidences of having the Holy Spirit. The Holy Spirit, gives the believer supernatural ability, to speak in the different languages of this world—languages that the believer who is speaking, is totally unfamiliar with, and ignorant of that language. An example is on the

Day of Pentecost in the first-century church (Acts 2:1-12).

Interpretation of Tongues

This gift is the supernatural inheritance by the Holy Spirit that will empower a person to receive an interpretation of the message in tongues through a vision or through an inspiration. 1 Corinthians 4:7 reminds us the manifestation of the gifts that are given and decided by the Holy Spirit. Believers are filled with the Holy Spirit. It is imperative that believers yielded their vessels to allow the Holy Spirit to work through them, in order for the gifts of the Holy Spirit to flow like a river.

CHAPTER II

SEVEN SPIRITS OF GOD

In a physical correlation with the rainbow around the throne (Revelation 4:3), we know that the colors in a rainbow are seven. One can recognize the characters of God in the seven spirits of God, which is the rainbow around the throne of God. The rainbow appears to be a radiance around the throne. Remember Genesis 1:2, "God hovering in Hebrew (*rachaph*) to brood, to flutter that is a movement of a dove." This is an example of the Holy Spirit seen around the throne.

It is vital that the believer correlates the seven Spirits of God with the nine spiritual gifts from the Holy Spirit. As mentioned before, all believers can manifest the nine gifts of the Holy

Spirit as He distributes them. However, the Seven Spirits of God are for seasoned believers who have yielded their spirit, soul, and body unto the Holy Spirit. It is God's pleasure to pour out His Seven Spirits upon His Church (Ezekiel 37:1-10).

The Seven Spirits of God are mentioned two times (Revelation 4:5; 5:6 and Revelation 1:4; 3:1). Further, in the book of Isaiah 11:2, it mentions all of the seven spirits of God:

1. The Spirit of the Lord
2. The Spirit of Wisdom
3. The Spirit of Understanding
4. The Spirit of Counsel
5. The Spirit of Might
6. The Spirit of Knowledge
7. The Spirit of the Fear of the Lord

The above seven spirits work in groups of two's. Isaiah the prophet wrote about them in pairs. However, they operate in four groups:

1. The Spirit of the Lord (Class by itself)
2. Spirit of Wisdom & Understanding/ Revelation
3. Spirit of Counsel & Might
4. Spirit of Knowledge & of the Fear of the Lord

With the above seven spirits, the five–fold Minister must seek and ask Jesus Christ for the Spirits to rest upon them. Still, it is determined by Jesus Christ and the Holy Spirit who will receive the spirits of God and not man. Their prayers can focus on earnestly seeking God with sincere heart-felt prayers, continually until they manifest. Prayer to God includes asking Him to remove anything in you that does not make you worthy of the seven spirits of God.

The Spirit of the Lord

The Holy Spirit manifests Himself as the Spirit of Christ. In (2 Corinthians 3:17) Now the Lord is the Spirit, and where the Spirit of the Lord is, there is freedom.

The Holy Spirit dwells in you and represents Jesus Christ manifesting Himself in His people (Romans 8:9). But you are not controlled by your sinful nature. You are controlled by the Spirit if you have the Spirit of God living in you. (And remember that those who do not have the Spirit of Christ living in them do not belong to him at all).

With regard to the Spirit of the Lord, the word 'Spirit' in Hebrew is *ruwach* *meaning* breath; strength, wind, breeze, spirit (or Spirit), a violent exhalation, a violent blast of the breath of God.

The Spirit of the Lord is the manifest presence of the Holy Spirit. His manifest presence is like a thick cloud that comes down to rest. When the nine gifts are demonstrated by the anointing of the Holy Spirit (1Corinthians 12:8-10) and the Spirit of the Lord is the manifest presence of the Holy Spirit it requires no anointing (Exodus 33:13-18). Here are some of the forms of the presence of the Holy Spirit; His Shekinah Glory Cloud (2 Chronicles 5:13-14), the Dove (Luke 3:21-22), the River of Living Water (John 7:38-39), The Mighty Wind (Acts 2:1-4), The Menorah (Revelation 4:5), the Flood (Isaiah 59:19) and the

Spirit of Christ (Romans 8:9) remember He is not limited to this list.

The Spirit of the Lord operates with the all of the nine gifts and flows like a river in four different directions (Genesis 2:10-14; Ezekiel 47:3-5).

The keys to flow with the Holy Spirit are obedience (Isa 63:10), faithfulness in what God has given you to do and meekness and humility; pride will bring destruction upon a person. The anointing will increase in the believer's life as they continue to humble themselves. Then God will promote you because He knows what's in the heart of every man.

Spirit of Wisdom & Understanding/Revelation
The Spirit of Wisdom and understanding or revelation is the supernatural empowerment of God

that ministers to the human spirit to remove the veil from believers' spirits so that they may know Jesus Christ. Also, it is purposed to obtain spiritual understanding and knowledge/revelation of the word of God. It reveals to the believer how to do things and when to do things in all situations. It also enhances the believers God-given abilities in order to demonstrate God's kingdom on earth.

That the God of our Lord Jesus Christ, the Father of glory, may give to you a spirit of wisdom and of revelation in the knowledge of Him
(Ephesians 1:17 NAS).

This scripture mentions revelation, but in Isaiah it indicates understanding. However in the Hebrew, revelation and understanding are the same.

The Spirit of Wisdom implies wholeness of wisdom. Wisdom in Hebrew *"chokmah"* means skill that comes from *Chokmah* a primitive root word *chakam* meaning "to be wise (in mind, word or act) or to deal wisely, make wiser. In the Greek wisdom is known as *Sophia,* meaning the insight into the true nature of things. Revelation," is discernment conveyed to the believer's spirit from the Holy Spirit and then transmitted to our hearts and our heads in this process.

Operation

Paul was taught by the spirit of wisdom and revelation (1Corinthians 11:23). Through the gift of vision and revelations, the elementary way the Spirit of Wisdom and Understanding/Revelation manifests is through a plethora of visions and revelations (2 Corinthians 12:1,7).

The spiritual gifts word of wisdom, word of knowledge and discerning of spirits manifests in the Spirit of Wisdom and Understanding/Revelation. It is essential that these three spiritual gifts operate with the spirit of wisdom and understanding/ revelation. When the Spirit of wisdom is resting upon a believer the three spiritual gifts become fixed residents within them.

The Spirit of Counsel and the Spirit of Might

The word counsel meaning in Hebrew is *etsah* which also means "advice or plan." Counselor in Hebrew is 'yo"es' that means "to advice, give counsel, determine or guide." However, when you combine the two together; advice and counsel, it is the Spirit of Counsel. The Spirit of Counsel is described as guidance or advice from the Holy Spirit; counseling manifests action from a plan.

The Spirit of Might

The word might in Hebrew is *'gebuwrah'* which means "force or power." The primary meaning of the word might is power/strength that implies acts of power/strength. The name of this Spirit of Might defines the meaning within itself establishing it as a mighty power of God (Deuteronomy 3:34; 2 Chronicles 20.6).

When combined together; the Spirit of Counsel and Might, the Holy Spirit will give the believer instructions on how to interact with the works of God.

When God's Spirit of Counsel pulls from the Spirit of wisdom it manifest mighty acts; a miracle (Job 36:9). The prerequisite is obedience; to obey the Holy Spirit's instruction in counseling before the mighty acts can manifest (1 King

GIFTS WITHIN THE GIFT

18:20-40; Jn 5:19-20; 8:28). The Spirit of Counsel and Might operate through Jesus Christ (Acts 23:11) and the Holy Spirit (Acts 8:29-40), angels Joshua 5:13-15). When the two flow as one there is a powerful explosion that takes place. This powerful, explosion manifests as a nuclear melting which demonstrates the greatness of His power. There are three words in Greek that display the power and might of power *dunamis, kratos,* and *ischus.*

Dunamis (Acts 3:1-9)

This word "power" in Greek is *dunamis,* meaning *"force, miraculous power, ability, might, (worker of) miracle, power, strength, violence and mighty (wonderful) work."*

Kratos (Acts 19:20)

"Power" is kratos, meaning *"vigor, dominion, might, power and strength."*

139

Ischus (James 5:16)

The word "mighty" in Greek is *ischus,* meaning "force: ability, might and power"

Soaking in the presence of Jesus Christ indicates the believer is spending time with Him and being alone with Him. Here are two key scriptures that flow in the Spirit of Counsel and Might.

Now when they saw the boldness of Peter and John and perceived that they were unlearned and ignorant men, they marveled; and they took knowledge of them, that they had been with Jesus (Act 4:13).

One day Jesus was teaching, and Pharisees and teachers of the law were sitting there. They had come from every village of Galilee and from Judea and Jerusalem. And the power of the Lord was with Jesus to heal the sick (Luke 5:16-17).

The Spirit of Knowledge and Fear of God
Spirit of Knowledge

The word 'knowledge in Hebrew means *da'ath* coming from the verb *yada* that means know. Pursuing this further, the English word 'to know' has the connotation of instruction, punishment, comprehension and discerning. There are two standards of knowledge; *Ginosko and Oida (Num 24:16, KJV)*. *Ginosko* knowledge means to have progressive knowledge and *Oida* knowledge means fullness. In essence, these words mean to have seen or perceived; to know, to have knowledge of whether absolutely, or divine knowledge.

Let's make this clear. The word 'knew' in Hebrew is yada which is growing into an intimate knowing of God. Knowledge is 'da'ath knowledge of God which is progressively. On this Christian journey believers are aware of God. This awareness of steadily seeking Him leads us into an intimate relationship with Him. The Spirit of Knowledge imparts instruction for comprehension of God and discerning of men's hearts; one in the knowledge of God and the knowledge of men.

Spirit of the Fear of the Lord

Fear in Hebrew is *yir'ah* which means morally, reverence, fearful and afraid; to be afraid, stand in awe. This scripture below describes the reverential fear that is mixed with love and respect.

While Jesus was here on earth, he offered prayers and pleadings, with a loud cry and tears, to the one who could rescue him from death. And God

GIFTS WITHIN THE GIFT

heard his prayers because of his deep reverence for God (Hebrew 5:7 NLT).

In the Greek there are two words that represent *fear*:

1. *Phobos* which means reverential fear, a wholesome dread of displeasing God. Liken to the English word fear represents phobia.

2. *Eulabeia* a holy fear which combines love with fear.

Spirit of the Fear of the Lord is the working of the Holy Spirit that yields a reverential holy fear of God. Both the Spirit of knowledge & Fear of God is the working of the Holy Spirit, which imparts an understanding of the knowledge of God and the ability to discern men that manifests as a reverential fear of God. The believer's spiritual eyes are open, the eyes of their understanding to see God, to know God and discern men hearts and

GIFTS WITHIN THE GIFT

revealing their secrets would not this demonstrate the fear of God (Acts 5:1-11).

The flow of the two spirits is progressive as they increase in ways according to your spiritual growth. Just like a person must begin to crawl before they walk and walk before they run the same happens in the spirit, it is progressive (Proverbs 9:10).The Spirit of Knowledge brings understanding (Proverbs 2:5) and understanding brings the fear of God (Proverbs 1:7). And knowledge of God comes by speaking in tongues (Acts 2:7-11).

When discussing matters of the Spirit of Knowledge and the Fear of the Lord through the gifts of prophecy, tongues and interpretation of tongues the knowledge of God comes by speaking in tongues (Acts 2:7-11) and the gift of Prophecy works together with speaking in tongues

(1Corinthians 14:22-25) to produce the same. Operation through the Spirit of knowledge and fear of the Lord is through Jesus Christ happens by being full of the word of God (Colossians 3;16), walking in the fear of God (Ecclesiastes 12:13), guarding secrets (Deuteronomy 29:29) and praying in tongues (Jude 20).

The Holy Spirit gives believing five-fold ministers the ability to sustain the Seven Spirits of God and the nine spiritual gifts.

Here's a list below that would aid them in preserving the gifts and the seven Spirits of God with the help of the Holy Spirit and this list is not written in stone more could be added.

• Be pure, clean and holy (Daniel 1:8)
• Delight in God (Provers 8:30-31)
• Be Humble like a little child (Luke 10:21)

145

- Meditate on the Word of God (Joshua 1:8)
- Learn to Wait on God (Proverbs 8:34-35)

CHAPTER 12

THE PURPOSE OF THE GIFTS

There are 7 purposes of the gifts. They are:

4. To declare Jesus as Lord (Acts 1:8; Acts 3-4:12).

5. To establish God's presence among us (1 Corinthians 14:25).

6. To set the captives & oppressed free (Luke 4:18-19).

7. To be the justification of ministries (2 Corinthians 12:12).

8. To illustrate God's power (Genesis 1:26, 28).

9. To confirm the Holy Spirit (1 Corinthians 12:7).

When the presence of God manifests, all things are possible. Warning and words of caution do not reduce ministry to their gifts.

Remember the gifts are used to manifest the breath of God that is within you and upon you for the purpose of demonstrating the supernatural kingdom of God on the earth. That makes you a sign and a wonder in the earth so refuse to diminish God and his power.

CHAPTER 13

THE BODY OF CHRIST IS A PARTICIPANT IN THE PLANS OF GOD

Throughout this book, the gifts of the Holy Spirit are given for the general good of every Christian. It is not imparted for the personal profit of anyone but for the edification of others (Matthew 10:8). Every believer in the Body of Christ is a participant in the plans of God. As such, the Holy Spirit apportions the gifts to each person (whether they are spiritually young or old) as He wills (1 Corinthians 12:11).

CHAPTER 14

PRAYING IN TONGUES

My sister and I have trained all over the country and have found out there are many believers that don't understand tongues or do not speak in tongues. So this section is dedicated to help ing the believer understand praying in tongues, and why they need to be filled with the Holy Spirit. Praying in tongues is like water; humanity needs water to survive. Believers need praying in tongues to become victorious in this Christian walk.

Praying in tongues is also referred as praying in the spirit or one's personal prayer language. This is a spiritual language used for the

GIFTS WITHIN THE GIFT

following: Private prayer, for he who speaks in a tongue does not speak to men but to God, for no one understands him; however, in the spirit, He speaks mysteries (1 Corinthians 14.2).

Personal Edification

Personal edification is for you to improve yourself spiritually, building up your soul and spirit (Jude 20:1).

Intercession

Believer's who send intercessory prayers to intercede for all humanity as mentioned in 1 Timothy 2 :1-3, "Therefore I exhort first of all that supplication, prayers, intercessions, and giving of thanks be made for all men." In the same way, the Spirit also helps our weakness; for we do not know how to pray as we should, but the Spirit Himself intercedes for us with groaning's too deep for words; and He who searches the hearts knows what the mind of the Spirit is, because He intercedes for the saints according to the will of God. (Romans 8:26-27)

Worship in Tongues

Singing in tongues is a form of worship, it can catapult you to heights of worship. When you pray in the Spirit, pray with your mind also. Sing praise with your spirit and with your mind also. Otherwise, if you give thanks with your spirit praying in tongues, how can anyone that positions themselves as an outsider say, "Amen" to your thanksgiving when he/she does not know what you are saying? Your thanks are received by God but the other person is not being built up, 1 Corinthians 14:15-17 ESV.

Our spirit prayers

God created man/woman and we all have a body, soul, and spirit. When we pray in the spirit it is the Holy Spirit praying through our regenerated spirit in tongues. Praying and singing with our spirit implies using the gift of tongues.

Paul speaks of our spirit prayers when he is speaking about "praying in tongues" in Corinthians 14:14, "praying with the spirit," as in singing with the spirit or blessing in the spirit' can be found in 1 Corinthians 14:15-16.

Other than the gift of speaking in tongues, this private use of our spirit prayers (in tongues) does not need interpretation since it's addressed to God and not to men. For one who speaks in a tongue does not speak to men but to God (1 Corinthians 14:2).

Purpose in praying in tongues

It is the human spirit of man (not his mind, will or emotions) praying to God as described in Acts 2:4, "And they were all filled with the Holy Ghost, and began to speak with other tongues, as the Spirit gave them utterance."

Activate our spirit

When we pray in tongues we activate our spirit giving it room to connect with God which makes us sensitive to God's presence by putting our attention and focus on God. We press into His presence when we are built up and our perspective changed. We can sing and pray with our minds without using the spirit, being anywhere on this planet still focused on God. But we cannot pray in the spirit without using the Spirit.

God's love

Praying and singing with our spirit implies using the gift of tongues. This can help release the mysteries of God and ignite our hearts with passion and love for God.

Praying in the spirit connects us more to the love of God because as we pray we begin to realize that we are His children. According to the Bible, the gifts are motivated by love.

Divine revelation

God will give an insight or foresight on His plans and purposes when we pray in tongues. Many people say praying in the spirit or praying in tongues is the same. Praying in tongues is speaking mysteries. According to 1 Corinthians 14:2, we will receive divine revelation from God which is prophetic knowledge.

When you can't find words to pray

When we are praying a long time, we can run out of words to pray. However praying in the spirit gives us a reservoir of sounds and words by the Holy Spirit. In the same way, the Spirit also helps our weakness; for we do not know how to pray as we should, but the Spirit Himself intercedes for *us* with groaning's too deep for words (Roman 8:26).

Pray without ceasing

Praying without ceasing enables us to pray whenever and wherever we are and we can also do it while being busy with other things (1 Thessalonians. 5:17).

Praises

As the body of Christ gives God thanks through praying and singing in tongues, these praises pass through the flesh and limits of our minds and understanding. Once there is a breakthrough, it's the Spirit of God that is praying or singing back to God who is pouring out His love through us as we yield.

Let's not forget that praise is the entrance of God presence. Also, worshiping Him in singing in the spirit/tongues reveals God's holiness, His glory, and presence.

Overcoming evil thoughts

Sometimes our mind wanders. Other times thoughts can come to our mind that are not of God. Praying in the spirit then helps us to focus on Jesus! Praying in the spirit helps to quiet down our minds and come into alignment with God. For if I pray in tongues, my spirit prays, but my mind is unfruitful (1 Corinthians. 14:14)

Praying in the spirit/tongues eliminates pride from our lives, due to fact that it bypasses our intellect. That is why it is a necessity to pray in unknown tongues trusting in the Holy Spirit and according to Jude, it builds you up spiritually.

The Bible states that all can prophesy and be filled the Holy Spirit, Joel 2:28 and 1 Corinthians 14:31. Now I wish that all spoke in tongues, but even more that you would prophesy 1 Corinthians 14:5.

Personal edification

Praying in the Spirit is building you up in the spirit. Build you, beloved, building yourselves up in your most holy faith and praying in the Holy Spirit. Jude 20.

It does take all of that *(praying in tongues)*

All through our Christian walk, we have heard that it does not take all of that, (praying in tongues). If Paul prayed in tongues more than all the Corinthians together 1 Corinthians 14:18, than how much more do we need to do it. It *does* take all of that and more!

Praying in tongues is beneficial

Looking at these benefits and being edified in our walk with God is an awesome benefit. This confirms our desperate need for praying in tongues.

God does not hold back

God does not hold back his gifts from those who want to pray in tongues. Often there are just wrong expectations, ideas, doubts, un-forgiveness, fears that keep people from stepping into it.

In our ministry around the country, we have experienced people wanting the in-dwelling of the Holy Spirt with one of the evidences of speaking in tongues but have been unable to manifest it. From our experience people who have not forgiven others can cause hindrances in receiving the baptism of the Holy Spirit and speaking in spirit/tongues.

Requirements

As a believer all you have to do is ask and believe God by faith. To receive the infilling of the Holy Spirit, all you have to do is ask and have faith. Do you want to receive the infilling of the Holy

Spirit?   Ask God to fill you with His Holy Spirit according to the Word:

And I tell you, ask, and it will be given to you; seek, and you will find; knock, and it will be opened to you. For everyone who asks receives, and the one who seeks finds, and to the one who knocks it will be opened. What father among you, if his son asks for a fish, will instead of a fish give him a serpent; or if he asks for an egg, will give him a scorpion? If you then, who are evil, know how to give good gifts to your children, how much more will the heavenly Father give the Holy Spirit to those who ask him! Luke 11:9-16

The Word of God teaches that when the Believer is filled with the Holy Spirit, we speak with other tongues as the Spirit of God gives us utterance. It is the initial evidence or sign of the Baptism of the Holy Spirit (Act. 2;4)

You must have faith

If you are filled with the Holy Spirt, then praying in tongues is an ability that God has given us, no matter if you've ever exercised it or not, no matter if you're aware of it or not.

The Holy Spirit is a gentleman

The Holy Spirit will not force himself upon you. Obedience is stepping into it. When you want to pray in tongues, you decide when to do it, how to do it, how loud and how fast. The spirit is not taking you over but simply filling your mouth with words. However, when you want to pray in tongues, it is your part to take the initiative and open your mouth.

Tongues are a gift

It's a gift from God and He will never impose it on us and force us to do it. God's desired for you to receive the gift so you can build an intimate relationship with Him. It is up to you to receive the gift or reject it.

Chapter 15

Seeking the Face of God

....

Jesus's love propelled him to constantly trust and obey the will of God his Father. Jesus, the Father and the Holy Spirit are one. His desire is to please Him even until the point of death as a sacrificial lamb for the whole world. As believers we must seek God's face constantly for direction, help, healing, the gifts, our calling, our families, and so on.

We must seek the face of God, by having an intimate relationship through prayer, reading the word, fasting, praising, worshiping and meditation. This will allow the gifts within us to manifest through us by the Holy Spirit to help others as in the scriptures.

I have sought your face with all my heart; be gracious to me according to your promise. Psalm 119:58

As we draw near to God, He will draw near to us (James 4:8). God wants to be sought out, but He is also eager to reveal Himself to those who love Him. As we cultivate and honor this relationship, seeking the face of God becomes easier and easier.

For God, who said, "Let light shine out of darkness," made his light shine in our hearts to give us the light of the knowledge of God's glory displayed in the face of Christ. 2 Corinthians 4:6

God says that He has placed this light in our hearts to display the face of Christ. To seek the face of God, we need to dive into our hearts and find Christ there. As we think about whatever is trustworthy, good, noble, and praiseworthy, our minds are drawn into God's presence (Philippians 4:8).

Dwell on things above (Colossians 3:1-2). Let your mind meditate on heavenly things. Also, ask the Holy Spirit to help lead you into His presence. He is eager to help lead us to more of Christ.

As for me, I will be vindicated and will see your face; when I awake, I will be satisfied with seeing your likeness.

Psalm 17:15

God's Spirit that is within us, causes our spirit to seek His face because He's the one who created us. God is in complete control of this world, and looking at His face gives peace and security to our lives. There is healing for you ask you seek His face, God through Jesus, the gift poured out his liquid love in the form of His blood. His loves overflows into His expressions. Feelings of unworthiness and shame are washed away when we see and feel His love. God loves to spend the time with us, and we need the time with Him.

This is the generation of them that Seeks him, which
seek thy face, O Jacob. Selah
Psalm 24-6.

We are the generation. Generation meaning "all of the people born and living at about the same time, collectively." It can also be described as, "the average period, generally considered to be about thirty years, during which children are born and grown up, become adults, and begin to have children of their own." Also a group of individuals, most of whom are the same approximate age with similar ideas, problems, and attitudes, etc.

When you seek God's manifest presence, you are seeking Jesus Christ' face. "Presence" is a regular translation of the Hebrew word "face." faithfully, the body of Christ is to seek his "face." However, this is the Hebraic way of having access to God. Seeking his face is in his presence.

Let's look at an example of the scripture of the word search:

Proverbs 25-2

1. New International Version

it's the glory of God to conceal a matter; to

GIFTS WITHIN THE GIFT

search out a matter is the glory of kings.

2. New Living Translation

   it is God's privilege to conceal things and

   the king's privilege to discover them.

3. English Standard Version

   it is the glory of God to conceal things, but

   the glory of kings is to search things out.

Simply put its God advantage to conceal a thing
or matter and believers responsibility to search
it out.

These definitions imply a close and personal
encounter with the Lord Jesus Christ. We realize
that God is omnipresent everywhere and always
there (Matt 28:20) and He created all things. His
power habitually exists in maintaining ruler-ship of

all things. However, as his children, they need to yield to His presence. That is why the bible constantly indicates for the believer never to stop seeking the Lord; his presence.

When He's not with Us

When believers become depressed it is an indication that God's presence is not with them. Sure there are times in which the believer could not sense God's presence with them and they need to become tenacious in pressing into His presence. For this reason, the Bible repeatedly commands us to "seek the Lord . . . seek his presence continually."

There are periods when the believer can become careless and slothful in God by giving Him no thought and not trusting in Him. This diminishes His presence and the believer is then unable to discern His presence. In this place the believer needs to repent and seek God's presence.

There are times when believers cannot sense God's presence, like when David's sinned with Bathsheba in 2 Samuel 11. When a believer sins, they need to repent and seek God's presence.

God calls us to enjoy, acknowledge and be aware of Him at all times. This fleshly situation is always ready to overtake the believer. This is another reason why the believer should "seek his presence continually. God said, "My Presence will go with you, and I will give you rest. (Exodus 33:14)

What It Means to Seek

Seeking and setting your heart and mind on God is being cognizant of centering our heart and mind's affection on God. If then you have been raised with Christ, seek the things that are above, where Christ is; seated at the right hand of God (1 Chronicles 22:19).

According to Strong's, the Hebrew word **lebab** (3824) is rendered: "_heart_" (as the most interior organ); "_being, think in themselves_," "_breast_," "_comfortably_," "_courage_," "_midst_," "_mind_," "_unawares_," and "_understanding_." Strong's Greek Dictionary, states that the Greek word **kardia** (2588) is rendered: "_heart_," i.e. (figuratively), _the thoughts or feelings_ (mind); also (by analogy) the middle.

In both the Old Testament and the New Testament the word "heart" is used to refer to the whole of the innermost part of the human, NOT merely the emotions. Now in the twenty-first century heart is express as emotion from the physical inner of part of a human.

Biblically the word heart indicates three parts:

1. Mental action and reaction occurs,
2. Emotional reactions are felt and
3. Will, where optional decisions are made between rational and motive.

It's a choice for the believer to direct their hearts toward God. This is what Paul prayed on the behalf of the church. In 2 Thessalonians 3:5 informs the believer, 'May the Lord direct your hearts to the love of God and to the steadfastness of Christ.' The awareness of your choice requires an effort on the believer's part. However, to seeking God is manifesting His mercy and grace toward the believer. He desires for the believer to soak and dwell in His presence. "Seeking God is the awareness that He hears them and the confident that the believer enters into His presence.

God is not distant from His creation He knows them and He cares. There are obstacles that the believer must remove, which is still their choice, such as their own thoughts, busyness in their lives such as cell phone calls, Facebook, Twitter, TV, children, husband, wives, e-mail, texting, video web chat and so many other things that occupy the believers' time from God.

The heavens declare His glory. His word the Bible reveals Jesus Christ, creation manifest that Elohim existence; the believers can seek him and make a choice through that. God has manifested His grace, and spiritual gifts through the Holy Spirit there are a plethora of evidence of God's existence that believers can make choices on accepting Him. Seeking is an awareness of Him through natural means and continually setting our hearts/minds toward Him, in all our experiences, and of the revelation of Him.

Avoid Stumbling Blocks

Barriers in the spirit realm exist. This includes demonic influences that the believer must overcome in order to enter seek the Lord and enter into His presence. Believers must realize that it's imperative that they overcome anything that would hinder their spiritual growth. In addition, believer's need to be set free from any demonic influence; deliverance should be considered as a plus in assisting them to overcome. Some believers have an idea of what makes them receptive to God's appearances. Some know what causes their sense to become dull and not discerning the presence of

God. They believe in crying out to God and asking Him to reveal their hindrances. The great promise to those who seek the Lord is that he will be found.

When the believers seek God and plead with the Him for mercy in revealing those things that have been stopping them from fulfilling their identity, purpose and destiny. He can cry out "O Lord, open my eyes (Job 8:5). O Lord, pull back the curtain of our blindness. Lord, allow your mercy to manifest as it enlightens our understanding of knowing you better. As a result the believer experiencing His manifest presence. This is seeing His face while avoiding stumbling blocks.

Humility

In his pride the wicked man does not seek him; in all his thoughts there is no room for God (Psalm 10:4).

176

Pride is a great hindrance toward seeking the Lord's face. Therefore, humility is important when seeking the Lord. God has promised if you seek Him you will find Him and when He is found, there is a great reward. God himself is our greatest reward and Jesus Christ and the Holy Spirit are the believer's gift. Moreover, when we have our Savior Jesus Christ, we have everything. Seek the Lord and his Spirit; seek his presence continually!

There are times in our lives that we need to have an intimate encounter with God, due to desperate situations. Every person reaches a place in life that makes us cry out to God. If you have reached that place before, you may have prayed "God, if you are with me, show me you are here in this moment." Such desire for connecting with God occurs often in the Bible. There are many instances where biblical figures struggled in their relationship with God. So what does it take to encounter the presence of the Holy God?

We will begin with Moses on Mount Sinai. Let's take a look at Exodus 33:12-23 and 34:28, 29. The scripture says:

"Moses said to the Lord, See, You say to me, 'Bring up this people,' but You have not let me know whom You will send with me. Yet You have said, 'I know you by name, and you have also found grace in My sight.' Now therefore, I pray You, if I have found favor in Your sight, show me now Your way, that I may know You, and that I may find favor in Your sight. Consider too that this nation is Your people. And He said, My Presence will go with you, and I will give you rest.

Then he said to Him, "If Your Presence does not go

with us, do not bring us up from here. For how will

it be known that I have found favor in Your sight, I

and Your people? Is it not by Your going with us, so

that we will be distinguished (successful, respect), I

and Your people, from all the people who are on the

face of the earth? The Lord said to Moses, I will do

this thing of which you have spoken, for you have

found favor in My sight, and I know you by name.

Then Moses said, "I pray, show me Your glory."

Then He said, "I will make all My goodness pass

before you, and I will proclaim the name of

the Lord before you. I will be gracious to whom I

will be gracious and will show mercy on whom I

will show mercy." He said, "You cannot see My face,

for no man can see Me and live."

Then the Lord said, "Indeed, there is a place by Me.

You must stand on the rock. While My glory passes

by, I will put you in a cleft of the rock and will cover you with My hand while I pass by. Then I will take away My hand, and you will see My back, but My face may not be seen."

Moses was there with the Lord 40 days and 40 nights without eating bread or drinking water. And he wrote on the tablets the words of the covenant the Ten Commandments. When Moses came down from Mount Sinai with the two tablets of the covenant law in his hands, he was not aware that his face was radiant because he had spoken with the Lord.

God had just brought the Israelites out of the land of Egypt. As they made their way through the desert, they came to Mount Sinai. Moses had the task of leading the Israelites into the Promised Land, but this was a difficult job. Moses was under pressure. If he was going to continue to lead thousands of people through the desert, he wanted to make sure that God was going to be with him. On Mount Sinai, Moses asked God to reveal His glory to him. God agreed to his request but emphasized that no human could see the fullness of His glory and live. Moses witnessed the glory of God and it had an extraordinary effect on him. Those who seek God earnestly desire the same experience. So how do we seek God's face? How can we become witnesses to His glory? What can we expect to take place when we encounter the living God? It comes through passion.

Passion

The beginning for drawing closer to God is a holy desire to know God. Passion is born from a love and honor of God and His Word, thanksgiving for what God has done for us, and an awe of God's greatness and goodness. Passion comes from a choice to seek after God in the good and bad times, when we're strong and when we're weak. It was passion that propelled Christ to carry the cross to Calvary. Passion should lead to obedience and humility. Also, passion should manifest in holiness, without which on one will see God (Hebrew 12:14).

Scripture is filled with many examples of people who expressed their passion for knowing God. The writers of the Psalms demonstrated passion in their prayers. We can see glimpses of the beautiful pictures of passion painted throughout the Psalms:

As the deer pants after the water brooks, so my soul pants after You, O God. My soul thirsts for God, for

the living God. When will I come and appear before
God?

Psalms. 42:1-2

How lovely is Your dwelling place, O Lord of
Hosts! My soul longs, yes, even faints for the courts
of the Lord; my heart and my body cry out for the
living God.

Psalms. 84:1-2

As for me, I will see Your face in righteousness; I
will be satisfied when I awake with Your likeness...

Psalms 17:15

When You said, "Seek My face," my heart said to
You, "Your face, Lord, I will seek."
Psalms. 27:8

These passages also raise questions. Why would these writers want to seek God's face? They most certainly knew the story of Moses' encounter with God. They knew they could not see His face and live. It was their passion to seek God that made them want to know God on a deeper level, even being willing to risk their lives to know the God they loved more personally. And this kept them humble at his feet. During your next time of prayer, pray these verses to God and let Him know that you desire to know Him more deeply. It will humble you.

Passionate Prayer

When you are passionate for God, you want to talk with Him all the time. Most people know what it is like to fall in love with someone. When you want to know someone more intimately, you feel compelled to talk to that person as much as possible. I remember the early stages of my dating relationship with my husband. I spent time with him as much as I could. Eventually, I wanted to be with him so much that I decided to spend the rest of my life with him. This is the kind of relationship God wants with His people. He calls us His bride and He wants us to pursue a relationship with Him daily.

Moses spent 40 continuous days and nights with God. What did he do during that time? He talked with God. Sometimes our concept of prayer becomes over-spiritualized. It is not a magic potion we use to get what we want on our wish list. Prayer simply means talking to God. In the same manner, in which you can have a conversation with your friend or relative, you can talk to God too! If we want to learn how to pray more effectively, a good place to start is by studying the Lord's Prayer. We find that there are different types of prayer and that the right attitude should be displayed as we pray. Also, the Holy Spirit can teach the believer how to pray.

As being gifts we need to see the face of God like Moses. So many believers don't see the face of God because of spiritual blindness, and they allow the cares of this world to blind them. Moses is a great example of seeing the face of God face to face. In addition, we have to believe and see God through His creation on the earth, in His word, and through the Holy Spirit.

Since then, no prophet has risen in Israel like Moses, whom the Lord knew face to face, Deuteronomy 34:10. Moses spends time with God speaking to Him as one would with another person. He came out of God's presence with the glory of

God on him so much that His face shined. Looking on the face of God opens us up to receive more of who He is and to understand more of His intent.

As you look into His face He may tell you to be holy, but all of a sudden you no longer see it as a rebuke or an unreachable goal. You can see the tenderness in His eyes though His Word and the Holy Spirit. Now there is nothing else in the entire world you would rather do. And, you believe it is possible.

Just think, the experience of Moses is not the high mark of the Christian faith, but instead it is the baseline of what we are expected to experience. We can boldly enter the throne room of God Hebrews 4:16. We can fix our eyes on Jesus. Hebrews 12:1-2. Seeing the face of God is an experience available to every believer.

As gifts it is Importance of Seeking the Face of God

We must search, chase, and run after God's face and all His promises. However, the enemy will have the believer to think that they are unworthy to seek after God because of the things they have done in their pass.

Some Christians and some believers still have a misunderstanding of who God is. It is typical for believers to think God is disappointed with them. We are so focused on our sins and mistakes that we feel that God is shaking His hand at us. This affects our approach to Him. We bow our heads, we grovel at His feet, and we tell Him how unworthy we are. We come to God like the prodigal son with our, "I'm so sorry" speech, but we never look up to His face to see Him put on us His robe and ring.

We feel like Job when he asked God why do you hide your face from me Job 13:24? But like Job, God is not hiding his face. We can't see past our circumstances to realize that God is still there. He still loves us.

The Lord bless you and keep you; the Lord make his face shine on you and be gracious to you; the Lord turn his face toward you and give you peace, Numbers 6:24-26.

This blessing in Numbers has been spoken in the church throughout the ages as a declaration over the people. The power in this blessing is that it is in the heart of God to bless us and be gracious towards us. God loves us when we seek His face,

His face lights up because we are His dearly loved children (Romans 8:14-17).

And we all, who with unveiled faces contemplate the Lord's glory, are being transformed into his image with ever-increasing glory, which comes from the Lord, who is the Spirit (2 Corinthians 3:18).

Looking on the face of God transforms us into His image. We become like the things we focus on. When we spend our time in fear or worry, our lives are filled with hardships. When we focus on money, we become greedy. When we focus on our needs, we become desperate in filling them. When we focus on the things done wrong against us, we become bitter and angry. It is only in God that when we focus on Him that all the good things are added Matthew 6:33.

CHAPTER 16

FINAL CLOSING CHAPTER

Let us realize that our children are gifts also, from generation to generation. We release our children (gifts) back into the original intent God has for their lives; to become world changers in advancing the kingdom of God.

"Children are a gift from the lord; they are a reward from Him."
Psalm 127:3 NLT

You too are a gift through Jesus and you need to exercise your area of giftedness. You need to ask God to help you discover your gifts, if you don't know what they are. If you do know, than you need to be productive, intuitive, comfortable, influential and satisfied.

In confidence you demonstrate the gifts of the Holy Spirit through you in the market place, work place and any of the seven mountains. Religion is the first mountain.

There are a plethora of categorized religions around the world but the Greek ecclesia the Christian Church responsibility to reach the lost with the love and Gospel of Jesus Christ and expand the kingdom of God with the spiritual gifts of the Holy Spirit.

The second mountain is family, which should be the building block of a community; however, there are so many dysfunctional families. God desires the body of Christ to move out in His spiritual gifts to bring order and stability into families.

The third mountain is education, which they removed prayer out of the schools and replace it non-biblical principles. How much more the nine gifts of the spirit and other spiritual gifts are needed into the education system to re-introduce biblical truth and values.

The fourth is government that needs more of God true believers in government that are not afraid to manifest God spiritual gifts and walk in the authority that God has given them. In Proverbs 14:34 states "righteousness exalts a nation, but sin is a reproach to any people."

The fifth mountain is the media which is the radio, TV news station, newspapers, internet news and etc. This mountain has the ability to influence trillion of minds. One can image the Christian community over take the media and all the air ways are influencing trillion with spiritual gifts, spiritual programs twenty-four hours by seven days out of a week.

The sixth mountain is arts & entertainment demonstrating spiritual gifts that would influence our society, music filmmaking, social media, and television.

The final mountain is business, the word of knowledge, word of wisdom and the other spiritual gifts giving revelation from the Holy Spirit on how to create wealth will assist believers in the markets and the economic systems.

As a gift, pay close attention to what God tells you. Give appropriate attention to detail. Further, take responsibility for what God has entrusted to you. Regardless of your titles being a gift causes you to influence other with in a positive way; through the word, and living a Holy and righteous life.

We encourage the body of Christ zealously to chase after all of the gifts. Never, allow the enemy to manipulate you in putting gifts before the Giver of all gifts.

CHAPTER 17

PROPHET HELEN'S PROPHETIC HEART

My prophetic people get delivered from the spirit of rejection! Do you not know that I have accepted you? I have a set people which are called to you. A set nation, a set city, a set state. Did I not say that I have the king's heart and I turn it in what every way I will! So still your hearts and stay focused on me not looking to the right nor to the left!

In this time I am saturating you in my Spirit that you will move in power, to heal the sick, raise the dead to walk in greater exploits! Let unity be known among you. Let unification come with the Apostle, Prophets, Pastors, Evangelist, Teachers and the Body Christ!

Truly we were given the greater gift (Jesus) and from Jesus, the gift, gifts were given to us! So let us as gifts give our gifts to others through the gifts of the Holy Spirit!

Chapter 18

Prophet Harlene's Prophetic Heart

- -

Years ago I was preparing for a party. As I was setting up in my basement, plastic from some of the merchandise I had fallen on the floor in front of the fourteen steps. Within me, I heard the Holy Spirit speak remove that piece of plastic from the floor. I acknowledged Him by saying I will but got busy doing other things. The landline telephone rang in the kitchen. I said to myself surely, I am still young enough to run up from the basement on these fourteen steps and get the phone before the third ring. As I ran up the steps my left foot slipped on that plastic. The top half of my body twisted toward the east including my arms and I felt my body falling toward the west into the steps head first.

Something supernatural happened. I felt time had stood still. My body did not fall into the stairs head first like it should have. Something was holding me. In my mind's eye, I saw where I was standing and I watched my left foot turn from the side to flat as the top half of my body twisted from the east to the west. Finally, I got my footing and ran up the stairs before the third ring. When I answered the phone and said hello, a moving video camera starting playing in my mind's eye of what had just happened and tears begin to swell up inside of me. The thoughts came to my mind that I could have been gone (dead). I down played that supernatural occurrence because those around me had down played it also. I did receive a greater appreciation of life but diminished the power of God.

I mention this story to remind you to remember the supernatural occurrences that demonstrate God's power in your life. Build from those memories which illustrate God's supernatural manifestation. Like a snowball gets bigger and bigger memories can enhance your ability to expect and demonstrate the supernatural manifestation of God. Due to the fact that you have acknowledged God and his awesomeness, keep Him at the helm. When you give yourself to remember what God has done (Psalms 78:9-10, 11), refuse to forget the memories and stories of what God has done in your life. Refuse to diminish God's power because you did not share the supernatural occurrences. Don't allow people to down play them either. Never become like those in Psalm 78, they tempted God because they did not remember his power the day he redeemed them from the oppressor (Psalms 78:42).

Appendix

The Word Gift

A Poem by Helen Speights

Truly your life is a gift

which you will no longer allow the enemy to drift

or sniff you away from My purposes

You will shift and be swift

about My plans and purposes in this season

Lift up you heart and don't miff

as you get a whiff of the plans of the enemy

which tries to sift your life like wheat.

As the gifts from the gift (Jesus)

uplift and shift into new dimensions of My Glory

through My Holy Spirit!

Prophetic Book Cover Meaning

The Gifts within the Gift book cover was a vision from God. He had impressed upon Harlene and I To have the hands of Jesus which was is the Gift, with the nail prints. The symbol of the dove which represents the Holy Spirit and the gift box that is wrapped represents all kinds of gifts on the cover.

We prayed and ask God to help us implement the vision he gave us for the cover and our spiritual father James Nesbit the Prophetic Artist name came up. God used James to put our vision into art form and he came up with this cover, we thank God for him. Praise the Lord!

The revelation of the vision hands and nail print represent Jesus paid the price. He truly is the ultimate Gift. The Dove represents the Holy Spirit which Jesus prayed to the Father to release Him. Further, the wrapped gift box you see in the form of a cross shape indicates, the believers are gifts unto the Body of Christ. In the background of cover represents our Heavenly Father throne. Jesus Christ the Son, hands are out stretched to all that welcomes Him in their hearts. Holy Spirit desires the believer to submit and yield to Him for direction and guidance. Believers are the gifts to the body of Christ.

The colors on the cover are white, purple. The white which represent light, goodness, innocence, purity, cleanliness, safety, faith, heaven, understanding, beginning, humility, sincerity, protection, maturity, and holiness. The color purple/violet represents the royalty, it symbolizes power, nobility, luxury, it's associated with wisdom, and creativity. The color of gold on the bottom of the dove's tail indicates wealth, success, triumph, wisdom, understanding, enlightenment, power and glory.

Special Notes on Prophecy

Heb. nabi, from a root meaning "*to bubble up/forward, boil forward, to flow, gush forward like a fountain as from a fountain*," hence "to utter" Also, the word 'to prophesy' in the Hebrew is *naba* appears in all periods of the Hebrew language. "As you prophesy" it's more than the prediction of future events. The word *naba* is derived from an Arabic root, *naba'a* which means *to announce*, meaning *the speaking forth of God's word to the people*. Further, this concept is also found in the Greek New Testament. The word 'prophecy' in Greek is *propheteia* which signifies *the speaking forth of the mind and counsel of God* (*pro*, "forth," *phemi*. "to speak"). The other Greek word, *propheteuo* means *the telling forth of divine counsels; to speak under inspiration.*

Simply put prophecy flow forward from our spirit spontaneously. Our minds do not form the words it's by the Holy Spirit (Matthew 10:19-20: 2 Peter1:21). When one receives prophecy it turns out confirmation majority of the time.

Prophetic prophecies are like kisses from the King. There is personal prophecy God is speaking to us. There is prophecy that through the Holy Spirit gives us for others; this does include all aspects of life. All in Christ can prophesy but not all are prophets.

There is a different administration in the prophetic:

a. general calling (Act 2) God speak to us about us

b. Prophetic Gifting/Calling (1 Corinthians 14:1) God speak to us about others

c. Prophetic Office (1Cor 12:29) God-given authority by speaking to change in all the governmental office.

The body of Christ should remember that prophetic voice by man through the Holy Spirit is subordinate to Scripture. There should not be any add-on to scriptures.

Prophecy describes words birthed by the Holy Spirit into our spirit. Speaking to His people indicating your sons and daughters shall prophesy. Elohim desires to communicate to His people and He requires intimacy with His creation. We as children of God have the honor of hearing God's voice and being guided by His Spirit. The sheep hear His voice, and He calls His own sheep by name and leads them out (John 10:3).

It's imperative that the body of Christ learn to discern God's voice from man's voice and

Satan's voice. The only way they can do this is to spend time in God's presence. Then they must understand the different techniques in what way is Holy Spirit is communicating for prophecy through the spoken word rhema, the logos word, audible voice, vision, dream physical sensations or mental images, strong mental thoughts, slight impression and a still small voice. Also, the rhema word comes from the Holy Spirit to the body through the gifts; word of wisdom, word of knowledge and prophecy this manifest faith within the body of Christ. The saints become empowered by this faith to believe the impossible (Romans 10:17).

There are five prophetic methods

1. **The office of the prophet**

    (Ephesians 4:8,11) he/she flows in guidance, rebuke, instruction, judgment and revelation.

Also, activate the body of Christ into their ministries gifts.

2. Prophetic preaching

This is bible base, inspired by the Holy Spirit words that change lives and have an impact of precision. In addition, this is for the body of Christ and not just for prophets.

3. Prophetic Presbytery

This is a group of people that are established in the five-fold ministers or prophets. They confirm one's calling into the five-fold ministry by commission or ordination and just activation the gifts in the body of Christ.

4. The Gift of Prophecy

This not the office of a prophet it's a general calling, all can participate for the foundation of edification, exhortation, and comfort (1Corinthians 14:3).

5. The Spirit of Prophecy

As mentioned earlier the Spirit remove all limitation like the open ocean. This is a special anointing from the Holy Spirit to demonstrate his power.

The book of Psalms in the Bible is prophetic prophecy in song. All of the author's song under the inspiration of Holy Spirit being upon them. We love to listen too prophetic prophecy minstrel anointed that the musicians play today. As the worship leaders sing songs under the inspiration of the Holy Spirit. These prophetic songs magnify God's glory and manifest words that edify, exhort and comfort.

Finally, the word of God indicates in a command to earnestly desire the spiritual gifts; this demonstrates a more excellent way (1Cor 12:31).

The word "earnestly desire" in Greek is *zeloo* meaning, *to have warmth of feeling for or against: covet (earnestly), (have) desire, (move with) envy, be jealous over.*

Prophetic Activations

The word challenges the believer to covet or desire spiritual gifts and greater demand was on the prophetic. It's a known fact that every believer can prophecy because of Jesus Christ DNA is running through their spirits and it's a grace gift. However, the believer determination depends on how much they are willing in exercising prophetically. The believer matures in discernment by training their senses by exercising them in spiritual gifts. Remembering an exercise I would do in the early days of my training. When the news would come on and they would mention someone is missing, I would ask Daddy God if this person is still here on earth or have they pass on. I was amazed at the Holy Spirit accuracy about the individuals that were missing. This exercise assisted me in building up confidence in discerning God's voice.

Reality check: there is true prophets and false prophets. Also, true and false prophecies and Paul tells us to test every prophecy (1 Thess 5:20-21). Some people had a situation where they believed that God spoke to them and later they found out that He didn't. Even so, a person operating in the spiritual gift of prophecy can sometimes miss it.

Prophetic activation is to aid you in discerning God's voice from other voices. Also to build you up with confident because of practice you have train your senses to discern good and evil (Heb 5:14).

Prophetic activation exercises

Ministering prophetically one to another is practicing to hear God's voice and grow in the prophetic. The Holy Spirit minister to your spirit man (the belly) and then you release it from your mouth. The Holy Spirit may give you words, images, phrases objects, colors, scriptures, actions, impressions, and so on.

Activation purpose is to break down any fear, doubt, and ignorance that may hinder that believer from operating in prophesies. In addition, some believers have never ministered in the prophetic now they will get an opportunity to do so. It is imperative that the environment is conducive to the Holy Spirit which makes it safe and loving. Activation stirs up the believer's spirit man to prophesy, 2 Tim1:6 Wherefore, I put thee in remembrance that thou stir up the gift of God, which is in thee by the putting on of my hands.

Here are some of the activations we have demonstrated that are list below. In addition, we have provided the information below on other activation from Benjamin Schaefer and John Eckhardt's list.

This is a list of some basic activation exercises which are good to start with. They also resemble the most common way which God talks to us.

The majority of these exercises focus on God talking to us. We need to realize that by doing so in practice we are not limiting God but yielding ourselves to his ways. The believer can grow comfortable and confident in these activations. God is creative; He likes different styles that allow the Holy Spirit to minister through His people.

**Helen & Harlene' use some of the activation
below at the Prophetic Conference**

Activation of color

Asking the Holy Spirit to give them a color for the person standing in front of you but not the color they are wearing. Also, ask the Holy Spirit how does that person identify with that particular color? Then give them a prophetic prophecy on that. After that person is finished he/she would switch turns. They are relying on the Holy Spirit instructions and building confidence in Him.

Table Activation

There are six people at the table, asking each of them to remove something out of their pockets or their purses. Have them to exchange the item with the person to the right of them. Ask them to prophesy words of encouragement; comfort and exhortation from the item they received from them until each person had a turn. They are practicing in hearing the voice of God and gaining confidence in the Holy Spirit.

Soul Train Lines Activation

Two lines of people face each other. From the beginning of the line, each person goes down the line to give a prophetic word or prophecy from the Holy Spirit, until they have completed the lines. By doing this, they are practicing trusting the voice of the Holy Spirit and speed.

Heart Prophetic Prophecy:

One of the prophetic activation we demonstrated was to ask Jesus Christ shows us the heart of this individual we were prophesying to. The Holy Spirit guided and explained to us how to relate to this person's heart.

Bind man Activation

Believer stand in front of the people with their eyes closed or has a scarf tied around their eyes so they cannot see. Another way is having that person facing their back to the people. One of the volunteer swill come up behind then and tap them on the shoulder and that person will begin to prophesy to them. This activation helps the person who is prophesying to totally depend on the Holy Spirit to give them what to say for that person that has tapped them on the shoulder.

Activations ideas from Benjamin Schaefer

Principles are the same but the words have been changed.

- **Using Theme** Choose a theme as a procedure for this large /small group exercise (e.g. colors). Then everyone asks Jesus Christ what specific item within this theme the person on their right exemplify (like the color → blue) and then ask Him how does this relate to the person prophetically (prophetic interpretation).

Foundational questions you ask:

1) What color does that other person like ask Jesus that question?

    a. Why?

    b. What is the meaning of it?

    c. How is this related to the person?

    d. What is it that You want be to share with him/her?

- Some say this is the simple approach to begin in practicing the prophetic for people that never done it before and have the desire to do so. Many believers do not recognize the voice of God due to not spending time in His presence and there are three voices in this world, God's, men and Satan. Spending time in His presence helps the believer to tune into God and expect God to relate and talk back to them. When they ask in Jesus name about the color and what the meaning of it for that person is.

- **Biblical Theme:** Believers can prophesy about the books of the Bible Old-Testimony or New Testimony, individuals in the Bible, spiritual gifts (Romans 12; 1 Corinthians 12), five-fold ministry (Ephesians 4:11), psalm, four gospels, and twelve tribes of Israel (Genesis 49), and etc ...

- **Other categories:** Prophesying about fruits, cities, nations, animal, color, season, weather, movie/comic character, form of water, room in a house, building, country, continent, state, people and etc...

- **Scripture** – Prophesying the scriptures requiring of God for a Bible verse for that individual. While you are asking God for a specific aspect of the word in the verse that the Holy Spirit may give you to focus on for ministering it to that person. Also, remembering the basic questions above just change the item.

- **Picture** – Prophesying from a mental image, inner picture, vision, impression, open vision, night vision and animated picture through the Holy Spirit for another person. Requiring of Him wants does it mean and how do it relate to that individuals.

- **Emotional Feeling** – Prophesying about emotions ask God to let you feel a certain emotion. Then ask the Holy Spirit what it means for that individual you are prophesying to.

- **Physical Sensation Prophesying** – When you require of the Holy Spirit for a physical sensation and then ask Him for that meaning or who is the person. God focuses on body parts so He can manifest healing for that individual or individuals. We might feel a rapid light sharp pain in your left or right knee while praying for someone or just sitting next to a person. God might want you to pray for that individual knee and also give a prophetic prophecy to that person.

- **Word of Knowledge Prophesying** – Inquiring of God for a particular word or phrase for the individual. Words or phrases quickly manifest in your mind. Further, this can range from people names, streets names, street address, a number, one single word, a sentence, even a song and anything you did not have any knowledge about. Do not forget the basic steps in the beginning in aiding you in prophesying to the individual.

- There could be a literal meaning and a symbolic meaning.

- The Holy Spirit could reference the past, present (now) and the future.

- Don't get into Interpretation of the prophetic prophecy that is the Holy Spirt position.

- God / Holy Spirit loves symbolism, they are in the Bible but refuse to get out of line with them.

Note: You have Jesus Christ DNA in you. It's alright to share with them about the sensation you have in your knee. God will confirm through His Holy Spirt that they did have issues with their knee it normal to operate in the kingdom atmosphere. This activation will increase the believer's faith and demonstrate the power of God.

Activation from Apostle Eckhardt

Words have been changed but the principles are the same

- Give a prayer to that individual then give a prophetic word

- Healing prayer then give prophetic prophecy on healing

- Speak and decree over that individual in a prophecy

- Deliverance from anger or hurt and etc., through prophetic prophecy

- Prophesying from reading a scripture

- Prophesying from using items that are around the individuals, etc.

- Prophesying by seeing a picture, the Holy Spirit will show you

- Prophesying one word only

- Prophesying from receiving a sensation in your body for healing, or feeling something, like, joy, peace.

- Prophesying by giving thanks and release a prophetic word.

- Prophesying a Bible Character example Isaiah, Jeremiah, and Easter etc.

- Prophesying from the Bible Book like Psalm on words of grace, favor, etc.

- Prophesying from speaking in tongues

- Prophesying from music and releases prophetic songs

- Prophesying from a Bible creature example: ox, lion, eagle, mule

- Prophesying on mineral ruby, pearl, gold, diamond

- Give prophetic words on New things Mat. 19:16, New Season, New Doors,

- Give prophetic words by laying on hands

- Give prophetic words by piggy-back from the first person that prophesy

- Give prophetic words from hearing a sound and release that prophetic word

- Give prophetic words regarding finances to individuals

- Give prophetic words about the five senses like what you taste, hear, smell, touch, and sight

- Give prophetic words on tonight or today the Lord will say this or that

- Give prophetic word in the days to come, in the pass, years ago

- Give prophetic words what you ear, your heart, shoulders, back, hands, eyes, face, feet,

- Give prophetic words on the Divine names of God example: Elohim

- Give prophetic words on the Greatness of God

- Give prophetic words about trees and nature

- Give prophetic words on different colors

- Give prophetic words on current events

- Give prophetic words from a person gifting and talents

- Give prophetic words on the market place and the seven mountains

Testimonies of Activations

Two question for the believers that were at the Prophetic Conference for activations:

One: How was the activation?

Two: How did the activation make you grow?

Here are some of the participants responses:

1. Russell mentions all the activations were good. He receives insight from God and that empowered him to become stronger in prophesying.

2. James indicates did the soul train activation which was great. He relied on the Holy Spirit not on the natural mind. And he did not have time to think about it, you just prophesy.

3. Susan the activation made her grow in the spirit. You have to rely on Jesus Christ for a word and when you give it out your words;

you choose to believe God that word is for that person. In whatever area they need that word and she receives that as well that it is God.

4. Mrs. Howard's activation prophesying to yourself and recording it on your cell phone.

She mentions it was difficult for her to do that because of the things she was going through. These was her words 'I speak joy, I speak love, I speak freedom to myself and to be love'. She pause and started crying and then continue 'to be received by God and know, He created me just as I am. She just thank God that he let herself hear those things that was an encouragement for her. From all of the activation she practices, it gave her strength to move forward regardless of it being difficult.

5. Alice activation prophesying to yourself and recording it on your cell phone. It was not hard but difficult looking at yourself and saying things because you had to think about what God would say to you. As she was speaking the word of God to herself it encouraged her. Like she would want to do that more and she said it made her see herself in a different light. She was looking at herself as God would look at her.

6. Kim activation prophesying to yourself and recording it on your cell phone. God confirmed some things as I prophesied to myself. He helped me to bring down some strongholds as He was telling me to change.

7. Barbara activation standing in front with your back to the people, she indicates it was such a challenge for her to know that God will tell you about every single person when

your back is turned. She loved the activation.

8. A Prophet male, had informed us this was his first time ever seeing this at a conference the body be activation and used in the prophetic prophecy and it blessed him.

Finally, Helen asked how many people receive prophetic prophecies that were right on and everyone in that room raised their hands. One of our purposes is to train and activate God's people to recognize the voice of God in the prophetic through activations. Truly the gifts are within Gift.

Eleven Things to Remember

Every Christian has one or more spiritual gifts. Holy Spirit manifest them as He sees fit which is to benefit all (1 Corinthians 12:7). Also, it's one and the same Spirit, distributing as he decides to each person, who produces all these things (1 Corinthians 12:11). Remember to each one of us grace was given according to the measure of the gift of Christ (Ephesians. 4:7).

Receive your Gift/gifts and use it to serve one another as good stewards of God's grace of (1Peter 4:10). Remember spiritual gifts are open to all believers. Note that Spiritual gifts are not confined to ethnic groups or sub-groups of believers. The Holy Spirit disperses the gifts as He pleases to all Christians.

Without questions, believers can and have received more than one spiritual gift. Because some of the gifts overlap with each other, the number of possible combinations is great. Believer's demonstrated more than one gift due to the Holy

Spirit orchestrated it to coincide with each person five-fold ministry gifts.

The moment a person is born again/ regenerated their spiritual gifts may be given. However, the blend of gifts may be undetected until Holy Spirit reveals them through a slow process.

Spiritual gifts can be abused and neglected, but if they are received when you are born again, it would appear that they cannot be lost. I think about William M. Branham who was a healing evangelist who demonstrated mighty signs wonder, yet there were some character flaws that did not stop his gifts. Furthermore, the Corinthian church showed believers can be gifted but spiritually immature.

Remember spiritual gifts are not the same as the gift of the Spirit. The gift of the Spirit has been bestowed on all believers (John 14:16; Acts 2:38), and every member of the body is suitable this gift. On the other hand, the gifts of the Spirit, are distributed as the Holy Spirit decides to each person (1 Corinthians 12:11).

Very important spiritual gifts are not the same as the fruit of the Spirit. Spiritual fruit is produced from within; they are imparted from without. Fruit relates to Christ character His image; gifts relate to Christian service. The fruit of the Spirit, especially love, is the motivator and its context for the function of all the gifts. Paul statement is made clear in 1 Corinthians 13, that spiritual gifts without spiritual fruit are worthless they are the basic of spiritual gifts. Eternal is the fruit and temporal is the gifts (1 Corinthians 13:8).

By now from reading this book you have realize that spiritual gifts are not the same as natural talents. Natural abilities which everyone has demonstrated from birth is unlike, spiritual gifts belong entirely to believers. Not always the case, the spiritual gifts coincide with natural ability, which makes the natural abilities better due to the supernatural quality. Both are given by God (Jas. 1:17), and should be developed and used according to their purpose for the glory of God (1 Corinthians 10:31).

Remember all Christians are called to a ministry, but not all are called to an office. Ministry is determined by the Holy Spirit divinely given gifts and opportunities (Ephesians 3:7). Offices (e.g., elder, deacon, evangelist, and teacher) are recognized by man and appointed spheres of ministry within the body.

Believer's desire spiritual gifts in the church more than others because they result in a greater edification of the body. Paul exhorted the Corinthian church to be eager for the greater gifts (1 Corinthians 12:31; see 12:28-30; 14:5).

Remember *Charismata* literally mean grace-gifts you cannot earn them they are undeservedly given by the Holy Spirit. There is no basis for boasting in pride or envy it's all from grace. God created each member of the body of Christ to find their identity, purpose and destiny. The same standard applies to all, it is required of all stewards that one be found faithful (1 Corinthians 4:2). Work with the anointing God has given to you and don't compare yourself with others (2 Timothy 1:6), and also seek to please God and not men (Galatians 1:10; 1 Thessalonians 2:4).

Remember gifts are God's spiritual equipment for effective service and edification of the body of Christ and they are not for building yourself up.

Photo Gallery of Activation at the Prophetic Conference

AUTHOR BIOGRAPHY

Prophet Helen Speights

Prophet, Helen Speights is a wife to Eddie; they have three blessed children and three grandchildren.

Prophet Helen Speights is the founder of the Davidic Generation Outreach Ministries, services are held every other Thursday's and Sunday in Chicago, IL. In addition, she believes that this is the generation of those who seek Him, who seek His face, Psalms 24:6. Further, she was the CEO of the Medical District Prayer Group, which includes Rush University Medical Center, John H Stroger Jr., Cook County Hospital and many other hospitals and churches.

Prophet Helen Speights received her Bachelor of Arts in Theology from Canon Bible College and Seminary, Orlando, FL in May 2005. She is an ordained prophet under the leadership of Apostle John Eckhardt, and a licensed instructor of the Manual Ministering Spiritual Gifts. Furthermore, she is a covenant member of I.M.P.A.C.T. Network.

God has also blessed Prophetess Helen to be an author of *Live to Pray and Pray to Live* and the *Live to Pray and Pray to Live Workbook*. She is a prayer warrior who operates in the gifts of God with a bold apostolic, prophetic, healing and teaching anointing. Prophet Helen has ministered locally and internationally teaching and activating in prayer and the prophetic.

Helen's heart's desire is to see saints of around the world suddenly rise to the supernatural. As the Holy Spirit manifests in their lives, heal the sick, cast out devils, prophesy, walk in signs, wonders, miracles, and prophetic evangelism. Further, bring in the glory of God and present the living Jesus Christ to the multitudes. God has ordained her to set the captives free.

Contact
Website: www.helenspeights.com
Email: GiftswithinGift@gmail.com

Prophet Harlene Pruitt

Prophet Harlene Pruitt has been ordained by man and commissioned by God with a strong apostolic, prophetic and healing anointing on her life to help the body of Christ. Her passion is to assist the body of Christ in identifying their purpose, identity and destiny through the word of

God. Her mission statement has been to 'heal the sick, cleanse the lepers, raise the dead, and cast out devils' (Matt 10:8). With a servant's heart manifested over a twenty year span, Prophet Harlene has served as a prophet, teacher, preacher and intercessory leader. She also served under the leadership of Apostle Roosevelt & Prophet Mattie Simpkins at Christ Universal Mission Church. Further, she obtained prophetic training from Apostle Burt Seavey; who is now with the Lord. She has ministered domestically in teaching, preaching, MSG training and activating in the prophetic. Prophet Harlene has become the author of two books "Gifts Within the Gift" and "Affair Proofing the Marital Relationship."

Prophet Harlene and her husband David Pruitt fellowship at Kingdom Impact Center in Aurora IL, under the leadership of Apostle Patrick

McManus. She is the founder of Oasis Healing Temple Ministries in Plainfield IL, and works diligently equipping God's children to become kingdom demonstrators of God's atmosphere. She is a member of Prophetic Company Group One at Crusaders Church. She is also an instructor in Ministering Spiritual Gifts (MSG).

Prophet Harlene has earned a Bachelor's degree in Psychology/Christian Counseling from Liberty University in Virginia 2014 and a Master's degree in Theology from Canon Bible College & Seminary in Florida 2007.

Prophet Harlene Pruitt is happily married to David Pruitt with three sons and two daughters-in-law and seven grandchildren.

Contact

Email: GiftswithinGift@gmail.com

Mail: P.O. Box 1551, Plainfield, IL 60544

Reference

Eckhardt, J. (2016). *Prophetic activation*. Lake Mary, FL: Charisma House.

Eckhardt, J. (2015). *Prophet, arise!* Lake Mary, FL: Charisma House.

Eckhardt, J. (2009). *God still speaks*. Lake Mary, FL: Charisma House.

Hagin, K. E. (2011). *Why Tongues*. Electronic Edition.

Hamon, B. (1987). *Prophets and personal prophecy*. Shippensburg, PA: Destiny Image

Selvaraj, S. (2015). *On dove's wings*. Singapore: Jesus Ministries Pte Ltd.

Selvaraj, S. (2015). *On eagle's wings*. Singapore: Jesus Ministries Pte Ltd.

John 14:12 - AMP - I assure you, most solemnly I tell you,... (n.d.). Retrieved April 21, 2017, from https://www.studylight.org/bible/amp/john/14-12.html

The Gifts of the Spirit. (n.d.). Retrieved April 21, 2017, from https://bible.org/article/gifts-spirit (n.d.). Retrieved April 21, 2017, from https://www.christcenteredmall.com/teachings/gifts/word-of-wisdom.htm

Introduction to the Prophetic Ministry. (n.d.). Retrieved April 21, 2017, from https://yearningheartsjourney.blogspot.com/2011/05/introduction-prophetic-ministry.html

Schaefer B. (2009). Basic Activation Exercises – Activating the Prophetic. Retrieved from: *yearningheartsjourney.blogspot.com*

What Does It Mean to Seek the Lord? (2009, August 19). Retrieved April 21, 2017, from http:// www.desiringgod.org/articles/what-does-it-mean-to-seek-the-lord

Bolin, B. (2012). ARTICLES & POSTS, BRENT'S - Biblical Counseling, BRENT'S - Biblical Error, MOST VITAL ARTICLES, NOTABLE WORKS & NOTABLE ORIGINAL WORKS Thinking vs. Emotions. (n.d.).

https://

faithbibleministriesblog.com/2012/07/06/the-heart-and-the-mind-what-the-biblical-word-heart-means/

https://www.studylight.org/bible/amp/john/
14-12.html

http://biblehub.com/1_corinthians/4-20.htm

https://bible.org/seriespage/25-spirituality-and-
spiritual-gifts-part-2-1-cor-124-11

https://www.christcenteredmall.com/teachings/gifts/
word-of-wisdom.htm

https://www.christcenteredmall.com/teachings/gifts/
index.htm
https://www.christcenteredmall.com/teachings/gifts/
miracles.htm
(n.d.). Retrieved April 21, 2017, from http://
biblehub.com/   hebrew/3820.htm
https://

www.Stronginfaith.org, 2007,

http://www.allaboutjesuschrist.org/emperor-constantine-faq.htm

Pinto, C. (2012). Lamp In The Dark-Untold History of the Bible ~ Full Film Retrieved from: https://www.youtube.com/watch?v=AVOuQF4Lgiw

Gill, A. L. (1995). The ministry gifts: apostles, prophets, evangelists, pastors, teachers. Fawnskin, CA: Powerhouse Pub

Blomgren, David K. *Prophetic gatherings in the church: the laying on of hands and prophecy.* Portland, Or.: Bible Temple, 1979. Print